Nurturing Talent

Dedicated to the Memory of
Sir Alexander Gibson

nurturing talent

the national youth orchestras *of* scotland

the first **25** years

Colin MacLean

Foreword by HRH The Earl of Wessex, Patron NYOS

Chapter 7, The Critic's Angle, by Conrad Wilson

nyos
the national youth orchestras *of* scotland

MAINSTREAM
PUBLISHING
EDINBURGH AND LONDON

First published in Great Britain in 2003 by
MAINSTREAM PUBLISHING (EDINBURGH) LTD
7 Albany Street
Edinburgh EH1 3UG

ISBN 1 84018 746 8 (Paperback)
ISBN 1 84018 747 6 (Hardback)

All photographs courtesy of NYOS unless otherwise indicated

A catalogue record for this book is available from the British Library

Typeset in Baskerville MT and Garamond

Printed in Great Britain by
Creative Print and Design Wales

Acknowledgements

In telling the story of a youth organisation one must acknowledge the swift passing of the years and of youth. How the young players come and go! When a national youth orchestra of Scotland was first being considered, in 1976, none of today's National Youth Orchestra of Scotland (NYOS) members was born, presumably not even a Camerata Scotland player. Some of the original NYOS members are already senior players in professional orchestras or hold other posts of consequence and/or are parents of remarkably mature-looking offspring. Over the years, NYOS has been the focus of perpetually renewable energy. All those hundreds of talented students have been a source of great, recurring and reassuring pleasure, for which grateful acknowledgement is due from NYOS founders, council members, staff, and of course audiences. Countless people have helped the NYOS project on its way and many are identified in the following pages.

So far as this book is concerned, warmest thanks to our ever-supportive patron, HRH the Earl of Wessex CVO, who has kindly provided the Foreword. Also to Lady Gibson for approving our dedication of the book to the memory of Sir Alexander Gibson, to whom NYOS owes so much.

NYOS is grateful to Carnegie UK Trust for a generous grant towards the cost of this publication.

I am grateful to Sir John Drummond for permission to quote from *Tainted by Experience: A Life in the Arts*; to Evelyn Glennie for permission to quote from *Good Vibrations: My Autobiography*; to Secker & Warburg for permission to quote from *Daring to Excel: The Story of the National Youth Orchestra of Great Britain* by the late Dame Ruth Railton; also to my one-time colleague Juliet Clough, as to Neil Munro, editor of *TES* Scotland, for permission to quote at length from the article Juliet wrote in 1976 in anticipation of the propitious SNO Prom at which young instrumentalists performed.

To Mainstream staff for their guidance, tolerance and efficiency, many thanks.

To Richard Chester and Dr Norman Cooper, my thanks for the supply of detailed and up-to-date information on the workings and the finances of NYOS; also to Professor Donald Pack for access to papers associated with the founding of NYOS; and to NYOS staff for various forms of support and for providing all the information assembled in the appendices. To Professor Alexander Fenton and to the consulate general of Japan in Edinburgh, my thanks for translations. Several people have read all or part of what I have written but I readily accept responsibility for whatever oversights or mistakes are committed in the following.

To Conrad Wilson, my gratitude for Chapter Seven: I was strongly of the opinion that the story of NYOS required the balance of informed critical detachment, which he is so well equipped to provide.

One final dual acknowledgement – a personal one. To Christie Duncan, who did so much for music in Scotland in his years with the Scottish Arts Council (SAC) and to the late David Robertson who did so many good and great things – always quietly – for Scottish education, not least for NYOS. As is recorded in Chapter One, it was to those two that I turned privately in 1978, seeking their permission to edge the project unobtrusively forward. I am still convinced that without their quiet blessing NYOS would not have been created when or as it was. But of course it had to happen sooner or later.

Colin MacLean

Contents

Try, for a moment, to imagine your world without music; not just in concert halls, but also on the radio or television, in your car or the cinema, at sports events or military parades. Life would be pretty dull. Yet music doesn't just happen, like so many skills it needs to be nurtured, encouraged and developed. One organisation in Scotland has been doing just that for a remarkable twenty-five years – the National Youth Orchestras of Scotland.

Many hundreds of the nation's young musicians have benefited directly from the NYOS experience, which has allowed their talent to flourish. Indeed such is the success that the National Youth *Orchestra* of Scotland has multiplied into four orchestras providing more young people with even more opportunities to perform and to play a wider repertoire.

The story of the first twenty five years recounted in the following pages is not just about the young musicians. It is also about the dedicated team of staff and professionals who have worked so inspirationally to build the reputation of the NYOS so that today it is held in high esteem both nationally and internationally. This is the story of one of Scotland's finest national assets.

I have been lucky enough to be Patron of the NYOS since 1987 and have thoroughly enjoyed supporting the orchestras, meeting the musicians and listening to their music since then. Whenever I attend a concert two things always strike me. Firstly the enthusiasm and energy of the players whatever the music, and some of their repertoire is very challenging. Secondly, the spread and depth of talent amongst the players, coming as they do from all over Scotland and the islands. That is what makes them truly national orchestras with real skill.

All of which makes me believe that music is alive and well in Scotland and, as the following story will reveal, is being nurtured, encouraged and developed. Let's truly hope that NYOS will continue making music for many years to come.

HRH The Earl of Wessex, CVO

ONE

Preliminaries

I

Climate and Context

In 1980, Professor Kenneth Leighton of Edinburgh University, writing in *The Scotsman*, said that in the 22 years during which he had been teaching and examining in Scotland not only numbers but also standards in music had risen 'in a quite spectacular manner'.[1] This quite spectacular improvement had made possible the creation, in the late 1970s, of the National Youth Orchestra of Scotland.

In the 1960s and early 1970s, governments of left and right had supported a new emphasis in schools on the arts, which were then given the title of minority subjects. There were signs in music teaching of a new freedom, a wider tolerance, a willingness to innovate. In most schools, especially primary schools, the one musical instrument to which any attention or training had been given was the voice – supplied free to all and capable, in most cases, of producing impressive sounds with comparatively little expert tuition. But choral singing of the kind which had been encouraged by many school teachers had lost much of its popularity, especially with boys. Some pupils still learned, at school or privately, to play the piano, but after the Second World War fewer pianos were being purchased for use in the home.

New and diverse musical forms, accessible to the young on radio, television and records, were proving popular with pupils. Rock and pop were giving way to punk. Teachers in the new comprehensives, expected to cope with mixed-ability classes, responded to new challenges in a variety of ways, depending on their own gifts and training, also to a great extent, on the facilities available to them and on the aptitudes or prejudices of the pupils. The raw energy, or the 'revolutionary snarlings', of some of the music that appealed to many teenage pupils was seen by worried adults as hostile to society, or at least a challenge to authority.[2] Teacher–pupil match in a comprehensive setting was difficult to achieve.

In some primary schools the recorder held new dominance, while in others, creative music-making, for instance with tuned percussion, was being developed. Instrumental tuition, and consequently the establishing of school orchestras, had been facilitated by the increasing availability of instruments, some of them comparatively cheap – and of questionable quality – imported from afar. Secondary schools began to stage their own versions of post-war musicals, or perhaps Gilbert and Sullivan operas. For such productions, instrumental support, from staff or pupils, was welcomed. Some music teachers and head teachers gave priority to the development of orchestras; others, often for good reasons, did not.

Meanwhile there had been considerable improvement in the range and standard of public professional performances – orchestral concerts, opera and ballet – which meant that more instructors of quality were available, though not all of them to schools. At the same time the professional companies were providing groups of players and performers to entertain and inform school audiences. In 1971 a committee representing musical and artistic interests in Scotland submitted to the secretary of state a memorandum expressing a growing concern about the lack of specialised facilities for gifted children.[3] The gifted child was peculiarly placed in those years of what came to be called comprehensivisation. In the context of mixed-ability teaching, priority for the gifted, or indeed the encouragement of competition, was seen by some educationists to be undesirable.

In 1973 a working group was appointed by the Scottish Education Department (SED) to inquire into the educational needs of children with exceptional gifts in music or dance and to consider what facilities might be provided to meet those needs in association with an existing secondary school. The publication of the group's report coincided with political pressure, much of it from local authority councillors, who wished to see specialist provision in at least some comprehensive secondaries to match what was offered in fee-paying schools such as George Watson's College and St Mary's Music School – two Edinburgh schools which the group visited in the course of its investigations.[4] Some local authorities had till then been sponsoring the attendance of gifted pupils at St Mary's.

The working group's report was published in 1976. Its recommendations led to the establishing of units for the musically gifted: these were to be at Broughton High and Flora Stevenson Primary School in Edinburgh, and Douglas Academy, Milngavie. The report, touching on the problem of identifying talent at an early stage, acknowledged that much depended on the chance coincidence of a gifted child having enlightened school teachers as well as enlightened and supportive parents.

The role of parents was central to the development of instrumental playing, especially at a time when peer group pressures were increasingly strong. Instruments were provided by many schools for the purpose of detecting and encouraging early development but eventually most instruments had to be purchased by parents who, then as ever, had to find time, tolerance and funds for supporting the various stages of progress in the musical development of their offspring.

In 1978 the SED Curriculum Paper 16, 'Music in Scottish Schools', was published.[5] By this time there was a wish to identify the new comprehensive schools with the developing quality of musical achievement. The paper read:

> The upsurge of instrumental teaching in Scottish schools over the past 25 years has been one of the successes of music education, with school, county and national bands and orchestras providing thousands of pupils with rich musical experience, leading many to a lifelong interest. That instrumental instruction is an investment in community terms can readily be seen by the numbers of young people now in bands and orchestras throughout the country which only a few years ago were in danger of extinction.

The content, style and role of music education in schools occupied the minds of those who produced the Curriculum Paper: they listed many of the possible and generally accepted means and ends of musical education. They asserted:

> Music of some kind is a basic need of young people. Children must be fired with enthusiasm and led to accept it as a rewarding experience. Most of our pupils will later spend their lives in employment which is not particularly skilled or interesting. They must have some deep affective source of satisfaction and it is by its contribution to this satisfaction that education in music must be judged.

As in so many contexts, school teachers were, it seemed, expected to solve major long-term problems of the individual and of society. That school music should be judged by whether it ensured that pupils would in later life tolerate uninteresting working conditions was, to say the least, a questionable proposition. The curriculum paper, however, offered a reasonable survey of the countless potentials as well as the challenges and difficulties of music education in the new comprehensive schools, now made even more challenging by the raising, in 1972, of the school leaving age.

By the mid-1970s there was an appreciable number of musical ensembles at school, local and regional level, under the supervision of teachers, advisers and others, all with their own objectives and agendas, some with generously comprehensive aims, others primarily in pursuit of excellence, some eager to hold their best players where they were, others eager to extend the players' experience in larger orchestras or under tuition of higher quality, for instance from professional orchestral instrumentalists.

The Edinburgh Youth Orchestra (EYO) had been gaining markedly in strength, though with membership predominantly drawn from fee-paying schools. Some instrumental teachers aimed to have their best pupils auditioned for the National Youth Orchestra of Great Britain (NYOGB), which had been in existence since 1948 and had been appearing regularly at the Edinburgh Festival as well as in other parts of Scotland. The Scottish Amateur Music Association (SAMA), which had been founded in 1956, ran courses and presented concerts with its National Youth String Orchestra of Scotland and its National Youth

Brass Band of Scotland. New regions, not least Strathclyde, were forming orchestras. There were specialist ensembles, ranging from the traditional brass bands still strong in some mining areas to new jazz groups, such as the Fife Youth Jazz Band. There was, too, the percussion specialism, at school and regional level in the north-east, from which Evelyn Glennie was to emerge: the Grampian percussion ensemble featured in the new Schools Proms in London's Albert Hall. There was, however, no symphony orchestra to draw on the full range of Scotland's talented young instrumentalists.

In 1976 the Scottish Arts Council (SAC) received a communication from the International Festival of Youth Orchestras suggesting the formation of a Scottish national youth symphony orchestra, along the lines of the NYOGB, to act as host orchestra at one of their festivals. On Friday, 18 June, SAC and SAMA jointly convened a meeting of people drawn from a variety of musical interests in Scotland. The purpose was to discuss the possibility of forming a national youth orchestra of Scotland. In the same month, on Monday, 28 June, the SAMA-sponsored National Youth Brass Band of Scotland and the National Youth String Orchestra of Scotland were to join forces for a concert in the SNO series of Glasgow Promenade Concerts. An article by Juliet Clough in the *Times Educational Supplement* (*TES*) Scotland looked forward to this concert. The article contained noteworthy passages:

> For Mr Bradley Catto, adviser in music to the Central Region, who has been director of the National Youth Brass Band of Scotland since 1971, the occasion is in itself the first public justification of the new demand by young brass players to be taken seriously as musicians: 'Brass bands have suffered too long from a cloth cap, seaside image,' he says. 'It is about time we proved what we can do.' [. . .] The programme they will be presenting on June 28 is an impressive demonstration of the association's long-standing policy of commissioning special works from leading composers [. . .] Many of the NYBBS's commissioned pieces have since been adopted by bands all over the country, in spite of a certain lingering and deep-rooted distrust of fancy modern stuff among umpah traditionalists. 'Our players tend to go back with

new confidence and poise to their local bands, dissatisfied with the stuff written 50 years ago.' [. . .]

But while a schoolboy with a trumpet can find himself something of a hero, a child turning up with a violin case for his first day at a comprehensive can as easily get himself booted all round the playground, says Mr Tom Devine, director of the National Youth String Orchestra of Scotland.[6]

The Glasgow Proms event was welcomed by musical opinion in Scotland and seen by some as a step towards the creation of a national youth orchestra. But all of six months elapsed before a further meeting was held to consider the proposal for such an orchestra.

At the conclusion of a meeting in Edinburgh on Friday, 10 December it was agreed unanimously that the idea of a national youth orchestra for Scotland should be pursued, also that the possibility of forming an ad hoc national youth orchestra, to act as the host orchestra at the International Festival of Youth Orchestras in Aberdeen in 1978, should be explored. A committee was appointed with Mr Alex Soutar, of SAMA, as interim secretary and Mr David Robertson, chairman of SAMA and director of education for Tayside Region, as interim chairman.

Five months later, on Wednesday, 4 May 1977, a meeting convened by SAMA was held in Edinburgh. Mr Robertson said that the delay had been due to illness and pressure of work. The meeting was told that the NYOGB might attend the 1978 International Festival of Youth Orchestras in Aberdeen. It was confirmed that the original idea had been to discuss the formation of a national youth orchestra of Scotland without particular reference to a performance in Aberdeen; now the interim secretary should receive, from those present, some ideas on possible options, also information about interested people and about sponsorship. A further meeting was arranged for Friday, 17 June. (The title and therefore the abbreviation NYOS were not agreed until later but it is convenient, from here on, simply to refer to NYOS. This will in most contexts refer to the symphony orchestra, but sometimes to the organisation as a whole. In June 2000 the council decided that the title of the overall organisation should be National Youth Orchestras of Scotland.)

CLIMATE AND CONTEXT

According to the surviving report of the meeting on 17 June:

> the consensus of opinion appeared to be that the best way forward
> was the establishment of a NYOS developed by the initiative of an
> independent person or group of people strongly committed to the
> project and prepared to devote a great deal of time and unpaid
> effort to it. The support could be presupposed of an existing
> national professional musical organisation such as the SNO. The
> objective would be to raise funds through sponsorship and
> patronage for the appointment of a director and support staff, to
> arrange for the auditioning and selection of players, to organise the
> tuition courses and to arrange performances and tours. There was
> general agreement that a small group who had indicated their
> commitment to the project should pursue these issues further and
> report back to the main committee in due course.

Those appointed to the sub-committee (subsequently and variously referred
to as the investigating, investigatory and feasibility committee) were: Miss
Kirsty Adam, principal arts officer for Fife Region, previously assistant
music adviser in the region; Mrs Helen Davidson, a local councillor who
was on the Convention of Scottish Local Authorities (COSLA) arts
committee, also representing SAMA; Mr Colin MacLean, editor of the *TES*
Scotland; Mr Denis O'Riordan, who with his wife and family was engaged
in a range of musical activities in Edinburgh; and Mr David Richardson,
general administrator of the Scottish National Orchestra.

Miss Adam agreed to be interim secretary of this sub-committee, also
it was proposed that the sub-committee should appoint their own
chairman at their first meeting. The sub-committee met on Wednesday,
17 August and then held six further meetings, the last on Wednesday, 19
April 1978. The chairman was Colin MacLean.

The report quoted above was eventually prepared by the sub-
committee. Little mention was made in the report of the many
difficulties and tensions, indeed substantial resistance, which had
become apparent in the 12 months from June 1976 leading up to the
meeting on 17 June 1977.

Reasons were, in fact, forcefully voiced in opposition to the creation
of a NYOS. These may be summarised as follows:

Nurturing Talent

1. There was not sufficient talent available in Scotland to support a national orchestra of high quality, certainly not to compare with the NYOGB, which drew from a population roughly ten times that of Scotland.

2. An appreciable number of talented Scottish instrumentalists were then being accepted for NYOGB and thus gaining tuition and experience not available in Scotland: it would be a pity to suggest to them that they should join a NYOS instead.

3. Instrumental tutors in Scotland, whether private or in council or fee-paying schools, gained in professional reputation from having pupils selected for NYOGB: some of these tutors might choose not to enter their pupils.

4. The good work developed over the years at national level by SAMA would be prejudiced, if not undermined.

5. The local authorities, especially the recently created regions, had been establishing their own youth orchestras and those responsible for such orchestras feared that their hard work would be threatened by the creation of a NYOS; there were other orchestras, including school orchestras, whose conductors or organisers envisaged a threat from the prospect of a NYOS.

6. There wasn't enough money to finance all the orchestras now proposed: local and national government finances, SAC funds, also sponsorship funding were already proving difficult to secure.

7. For talented young instrumentalists who were already in large orchestras, one more tier in the hierarchy of big youth orchestras could involve repetitious playing of a restricted repertoire, when they should be gaining more experience in small ensembles.

8. Even the best young instrumentalists should not be devoting all of their leisure time to music: in addition to orchestral playing many were preparing for Associated Board examinations. They should have time for other activities, thereby having the opportunity to experience a truly broad education.

Arguments for a NYOS were, of course, also presented:

1. When devolution was much in the air why should not Scotland have its own youth orchestra, to partner and feed its seniors –

SNO, Scottish Ballet, Scottish Opera and Scottish Philharmonic?

2. The creation of a NYOS, given high-quality tuition (not then widely available throughout Scotland) and the experience of working with soloists and conductors of repute, should feed quality back into other orchestras.

3. At this stage and later, the role and style of the NYOGB were under scrutiny: there were, it was said, more able Scottish applicants than NYOGB could cope with. NYOGB had a reputation for some degree of snobbish elitism, which it was hoped NYOS would not emulate; NYOGB players were said to be predominantly from non-comprehensive schools. NYOGB adopted a policy of excluding applicants who were at colleges where they received orchestral training; this seemed somewhat perverse.

Until NYOS was fully established there were several levels to discussions vis-a-vis NYOGB. If NYOS were to be seen as filling a gap in the hierarchy of youth orchestras, this tended to imply that it would be second best, whereas NYOS should, some argued, be content with no standards but the highest. If NYOS, unlike NYOGB, accepted students from colleges this should not be seen as a sign of weakness but rather as a sensible acquisition of strength.

In the event, the admission of college students would not only add to the musical strength of NYOS, it would afford to college students the experience they sought of playing the major classical works and it would give younger NYOS players a useful opportunity to work alongside, and tune in to the attitudes of, those older ones who were on the threshold of professionalism.

The pros and cons outlined above developed clarity and varying degrees of support as discussion progressed both before and long after the meeting on 17 June 1977. Most of those who had come to that meeting (at which the sub-committee, above, was appointed) had in fact assumed that it was to be, in the Scots sense of the expression, a *greetin-meetin*, that is a meeting to wind up affairs, to greet (weep) at parting, all business done. The arguments against the creation of a NYOS, it was claimed, outweighed the arguments in favour. But the chairman, David Robertson, having helped initiate the idea, had not yet abandoned hope.

He sought some signs of optimistic consensus. Stimulus came once again from Alexander Gibson who, as music director of the SNO, had promoted the idea of the Glasgow Prom in June 1976 in which young Scots instrumentalists had shown such promise. Gibson (knighted in the Queen's Birthday Honours of June 1977) had authorised David Richardson to say that the SNO would be willing to provide administrative support for the early years of a national youth orchestra.

Gibson's lifeline made it possible for an account of the meeting to report progress with some modest measure of truth. Detailed mention of all the doubts and forebodings which had been expressed at the meeting was to be omitted from the sub-committee's eventual report. However, sustained resistance to the creation of a NYOS was to be responsible for the sub-committee eventually choosing not to publish any report of their investigations and conclusions: copies would later be made available as tactics dictated.

The unpublished report, after listing the barest details of the above meetings, outlined the investigations undertaken by members of the sub-committee into the experience, constitution and operation of existing youth orchestras. The investigations were financed by the Scottish Arts Council in a grant making up to £200 available for the purpose. At a cost of £195, Miss Adam and Mrs Davidson visited and reported on meetings with officials of the NYOGB, the NYO of Wales, the Merseyside YO and the Edinburgh YO. They were accompanied by William Webb, personal assistant to the general administrator of the SNO: Mr Webb, whose expenses were paid by the SNO, also accompanied Mrs Davidson to meet Mr Ian Barrie, adviser in music, Strathclyde Region, in Glasgow, to discuss and report on the Glasgow Youth Orchestra. Mr Webb then attended meetings of the sub-committee. These three also acquired extensive information on the operation of the International Festival of Youth Orchestras.

The Merseyside orchestra was of particular interest because, its management being firmly within the organisation of the Royal Liverpool Philharmonic Society, it benefitted from contact with a professional orchestra, the Royal Liverpool Philharmonic. In Wales a member of HM Inspectorate outlined the work of the NYOW in the context of music education in Wales.

In Edinburgh Mr Herrick Bunney, chairman of the Edinburgh Youth

Orchestra, and Miss Helen F. McTavish, its secretary, explained the history and management of the EYO.

At a meeting in Croydon with Miss Ivey Dickson, musical director of the NYOGB, and Mr Simon Allfree, its administrator, the Scottish group gained information about the workings, style and attitudes of the NYOGB. It was not until some years later that Ruth Railton would provide an account in some detail of the many obstacles, indeed the insidious animosities, which she had had to overcome in establishing the NYOGB from 1948 onwards.[7] The Music Masters' Association, representing directors of music at public schools in England, had had the distinction of refusing to join the forceful opposition created by the Music Teachers' Association, the Schools Music Association, the Musicians' Union and others. Among Railton's strongest supporters from the start, however, had been Mr John Dalby who, as superintendent of music to Aberdeen's council schools, had been responsible for remarkable musical activities in that part of Scotland. The NYOGB owed a great deal, in both its creation and its development, to Dalby.

The Scottish investigating group had to cope with no unpleasantness in their various encounters south of the border: they drew on others' experience, gathering a range of varying statistics about administration, student fees, education authority support, sponsorship, fund-raising, and costs of conductors and soloists.

Referring briefly to arguments for and against the creation of a national youth orchestra, the sub-committee's unpublished report said:

> At an early stage we had to consider whether both our thinking
> and the likely course of events in relation to the creation of a
> NYOS should be circular or straight. The circular approach
> would mean that constantly and repeatedly the sub-committee
> would be questioning the very concept of a NYOS, wondering if
> certain regions or regional officials would be supportive,
> wondering too if the continued existence or prosperity or quality
> of this or that orchestra, or type or level of orchestra, would be
> imperilled by the creation of a new orchestra which bore the title
> of National and which was eager to justify that title.
>
> With the straighter approach the sub-committee would see the

early creation of a NYOS as the appropriate goal of our thinking and activities, so we would take advice on constitution, organisation, funding, sponsorship, recruitment etc, in order to see whether and in what way that goal was within reach.

The members of the sub-committee were unanimous in choosing the straight course – perhaps not surprising in view of the fact that we had been appointed because of our commitment to the idea of a NYOS. We felt that we should not explore again all the arguments already explored at the larger meetings in 1976 and 1977. We had been appointed to carry out a feasibility study: we thought that the best means of determining the limits and nature of feasibility was to think and speak in an affirmative way.

We agreed that the main stimulus in the creation of the sub-committee had been the suggestion by David Richardson that the NYOS might be brought into existence with administrative help and professional guidance from SNO staff. As this seemed by far the most likely means of bringing a NYOS into existence we felt that we should pursue the proposal carefully and fully. Having accepted the duty of investigating the possibility of sponsorship funding, the sub-committee realised that in order to stimulate response from others we had to speak in terms of the proposed creation of a NYOS rather than of continuing debate and of speculation.

The report concluded with an air of assertive confidence:

We do not here repeat or enlarge upon the arguments known to us for and against the creation of a NYOS, except to say that a NYOS of the kind we detail here seems to us likely to be capable of (1) commanding the allegiance, support and respect of all sectors, professional and amateur, geographical and social, of musical activity in Scotland, and (2) maintaining and developing a national organisation secure in administration, finance and continuing repute.

We believe that a NYOS of this kind would without difficulty gain a position of national stature alongside the Big Four – Scottish National Orchestra, Scottish Opera, Scottish Ballet and

> Scottish Philharmonic. These are, we feel sure, ready to support the idea of such an orchestra and would see it as nurturing much of the talent and helping to build up the public which they themselves require.

Colin MacLean's recollection is that the preparation of a report was thought appropriate, just in case its being available to a supportive few would be advantageous (as eventually it was); also, as SAC funding had been used, there was obvious propriety in preparing some record of the sub-committee's activities and findings. However, no polished report was published to join the noteworthy series of educational reports produced in Scotland in the 1970s. The committee merely agreed on what is above described as a straight approach; in reality it was an undeniably stealthy approach.

Permission was sought from David Robertson and Christie Duncan (music director of the SAC) not to circulate the report but simply to go ahead and see whether arrangements could be made for bringing an orchestra into being. Details could best be formulated at a later stage. Permission was granted, privately, by Messrs Robertson and Duncan.

In April 1979, the decision not to circulate or consult was to come under fire from members of Strathclyde Regional Council when it was reported that 15 of Strathclyde's best young players would be unable to take part fully in the International Festival of Youth Orchestras in Aberdeen because they had been signed up by NYOS, which would appear in the same festival as the Strathclyde Youth Orchestra. A total of 45 young players from the Strathclyde area had in fact been selected for NYOS. Strathclyde's deputy director of education, Mr Dan Burns, said that the proliferation of youth orchestras put pressure on some of the region's best players who were already heavily committed to local and national orchestras. Councillors said they had not been consulted about the setting-up of NYOS. The regional committee, however, agreed to subsidise those accepted for NYOS, but to do so only once, without creating precedent. The cost would be £4,500.

Mr Ian Barrie, music adviser in Strathclyde, had, as indicated above, been consulted by members of the sub-committee. But clearly there had been no formal consultation. The large and unwieldy Strathclyde region would present further problems in later years.

At a meeting on 30 March 1978 the sub-committee considered, among other things, the future government of NYOS. First, it had to find a suitable chairman. Colin MacLean proposed two names; a civil servant in Edinburgh on the point of retirement; and an academic in Glasgow. Glasgow was seen as more appropriate because of the intended SNO link, also because the man in question, Professor Donald Pack, combined some degree of independence from authority while at the same time commanding the respect of authority, for he had been chairman of the Scottish Certificate of Education Examination Board and recently chairman of a committee appointed by the secretary of state for Scotland to investigate truancy and indiscipline in schools in Scotland. Moreover, Professor Pack was actively interested in music both as an amateur instrumentalist and as a supporter of local and national performances.

Professor Pack, soon to retire from his post as a professor of mathematics at Strathclyde University, willingly accepted the invitation, and an exploratory meeting was held in his university department. When the sub-committee met on 19 April 1978, Colin MacLean explained that the sub-committee, once its work was completed, would be replaced by a new management group. This group came into being in May as a steering committee consisting of the original sub-committee with Professor Pack as its chairman. During the summer of 1978 it issued invitations to join a provisional council and, despite having no money as yet, pursued arrangements for concerts in 1979. It also met representatives of the Convention of Scottish Local Authorities (COSLA) in June to discuss ways in which local authorities might assist financially, and a suggestion was put forward – later acted upon – that two music advisers might be appointed to the future council. In all this work the committee was assisted by William Webb, who became the first administrator of NYOS. His partnership with Professor Pack over the next decade would prove happy and richly productive.

William Webb had been educated at Rugby School before studying law and modern languages at Merton College, Oxford. He spent three years at the Salzburg Mozarteum studying conducting, piano, bassoon and composition. A staff conductor at Trier Opera House in West

Germany for three years, he continued conducting on a freelance basis after joining the SNO's administrative staff in 1976. Webb continued as NYOS administrator until 1987 when he was appointed deputy director of the London College of Music. In 1987 he was succeeded by Richard Chester.

II

Foundations

The first meeting of the provisional council of NYOS was held in the Royal Scottish Academy of Music and Drama (RSAMD) in Glasgow on Thursday, 7 September 1978. Dr David Lumsden, principal of the college, was present as one of the council members. Professor Pack chaired the meeting, which was attended also by David Richardson (SNO), Herrick Bunney (EYO and St Giles'), Martin Dalby (BBC), Colin MacLean, David Robertson, Kirsty Adam, Helen Davidson, Denis O'Riordan, and William Webb as secretary. Martin Dalby, John Dalby's son, by then a composer as well as a BBC administrator, had been a viola player in the NYOGB. Webb and Richardson were also former members of the NYOGB, Webb as a bassoonist and Richardson as a trumpeter. Richardson was soon to leave the SNO and NYOS when he was appointed chief executive of the Minneapolis St Paul Orchestra.

Also present at the provisional council meeting was Mr Paul Pia (W. & J. Burness, Edinburgh solicitors) to advise on constitution. He had prepared a draft memorandum and articles of association for the creation of a company. Objectives had to be defined in order to secure charitable status. Several matters required early decision, including appropriate rulings on whether students need be resident in Scotland and/or be Scottish by birth. Martin Dalby asked whether full-time music students should be excluded from eligibility, as was then the case with

NYOGB. It was agreed that eligibility should in both respects be left as wide as possible from the start.

The provisional council was composed of the members of the steering committee and those invited to join in the preceding months. Mr Pia pointed out that it might be necessary for certain public bodies to be represented on the new council since NYOS must be seen to be representative of Scotland. COSLA had been invited to nominate representatives to the council, and it was suggested that two music advisers, one from the east and one from the west, should be council members. Directors of education, too, might be represented – as they already were, and would be until he retired, in the person of David Robertson.

William Webb had made provisional arrangements for a course and concerts in the summer of 1979. It was agreed that tutors of the highest available quality should be appointed. At this stage little was clear about the likely level or sources of funding: it was hoped that the Scottish Arts Council would offer support. It seemed likely that the Carnegie United Kingdom Trust might give £20,000 and the Hinrichsen Foundation up to £1,500.

The meeting of the provisional council ended after it was agreed that NYOS should go public as soon as £8,000 or more, further to what was meantime expected, had been promised to the orchestra. This was on 7 September 1978.

It happened that Colin MacLean had been invited to speak at a conference in St Andrews University on the weekend of 15 September. The theme of the conference (jointly arranged by the Nevis Institute and the Risk Research Group, London, Ltd) was 'Tomorrow's Scotland, Opportunities and Dangers'. At the introductory dinner on the Friday evening, Colin MacLean found himself sitting beside Robert Mennie, director of public affairs for British Petroleum Co Ltd in Scotland. These two had known one another as boys living in the same street in Aberdeen in the 1930s but had not met since then. They asked each other what now brought them together. Mennie said that in semi-retirement after a long career in oil he had the task of searching in Scotland for worthy causes that BP might sponsor. MacLean suggested that he and Mennie could, indeed should, help one another. NYOS needed £8,000 rather urgently, MacLean said. Mennie shook his head:

actually he was looking for a project requiring much more than £8,000. MacLean thought that was no problem. Within a week Mennie had met Professor Pack.

NYOS was incorporated as a company in Edinburgh on 1 December 1978. A press conference was then held at which the founding of NYOS was formally announced. Professor Pack received a cheque for £5,000 from the Carnegie UK Trust, the first instalment of a twenty thousand pound pump-priming grant. Further substantial financial support, Professor Pack announced, was expected within the next few weeks from a 'major international company'.

Professor Pack was now able to arrange with the SNO that Webb would be employed by NYOS for four days per week and that an assistant, Sandra Davidson, would join him in January 1979. Miss Davidson continued as assistant to the administrator until 1984 when Eva Flannery was appointed to the post. Miss Flannery has continued with NYOS. Since 1987 she has worked, latterly as administrator, under Richard Chester, the director.

The first NYOS course was to be in August 1979 at Trinity College, Glenalmond. The conductor at the concerts – in Falkirk, Aberdeen and Dundee – would be Nicholas Braithwaite, musical diector of Glyndebourne Touring Opera and chief guest conductor of the Norwegian Radio Orchestra. The associate conductor would be Nicholas Kraemer, who had conducted a number of concerts with the Scottish Chamber Orchestra. The second course would be at the New Year of 1979–80, with concerts in Edinburgh and Glasgow. NYOS membership would be open to young people between 12 and 21, who would be auditioned in February 1979, the size of the orchestra to be around 100.

By then COSLA had agreed to recommend to education authorities that they should respond favourably to requests by young people in their areas for sponsorship to the orchestra. The annual running costs of NYOS were at this stage expected to be around £35,000.

The first meeting of NYOS Council was held at the RSAMD on Thursday, 14 December 1978. There was now a councillor on the council (J. C. Campbell of Grampian Region) and two music advisers, James Clark from Strathclyde region and Richard Evans from Fife region. Lady Aberdeen and the general manager of the Scottish

Chamber Orchestra would be invited to join the council. It was affirmed that Professor Pack would be chairman of the company and Colin MacLean vice-chairman. David Robertson was invited to chair the Finance and General Purposes Committee. David Robertson continued as F and GP chairman till the mid-1990s: he died in 1998.

Professor Pack would continue as council chairman till 1988 when he became an Hon. President of NYOS alongside Sir Alexander Gibson. Colin MacLean succeeded Professor Pack as chairman in 1988, retiring in 1994; he has been a trustee of the NYOS endowment trust since its inception. Mrs Helen Davidson has been the longest-serving council member, having been in turn second and then first vice-chairman. Iain Harrison was chairman from 1994 to 2000 and was succeeded by Alan Simpson. Iain Harrison is now a trustee of the NYOS endowment trust.

At the meeting in December 1978 it was reported that the Hinrichsen Foundation had agreed to cover the cost of either the conductors' fee for two courses or the tutors' fees for one course, up to a total of £1,500. A firm answer on whether the Scottish Arts Council would support NYOS was not now expected until the Spring of 1979. It was agreed that the F and GP Committee should consider setting up a public appeal for NYOS (in fact, none was created). The chairman said there would be another press conference on 17 January in Glasgow, this time to announce details of sponsorship for NYOS from a 'major international company', which had already proposed that it would have one member on NYOS Council.

The administrator reported that 12 instrumental teachers had already agreed to be tutors for the summer course. He said he felt it would be incongruous if NYOS charged a higher course fee than NYOGB, which had recently raised its fee to £55. There was advantage, he said, in holding auditions early in the year, partly to avoid a clash with NYOGB which held auditions in the autumn – applicants could apply to NYOGB and if not accepted could then apply to NYOS. The council agreed that for the initial course an appropriate fee would be £50, and that local authorities be asked to pay the students' fees and also their travel expenses. In making this request it was to be pointed out that NYOS intended to perform and hold courses at venues all over Scotland.

Council agreed that if special funds could be made available a work should be commissioned from a young Scottish composer: John McLeod was to be approached.

Nurturing Talent

The identity of the 'major international company' was revealed at a press conference in Glasgow on 17 January 1979, when Mr Basil Butler OBE, a director of BP Petroleum Development, on behalf of the BP companies in Scotland, presented a cheque for £6,000, the first instalment of a promised £12,000 per annum for the next three years.

William Webb announced plans for the orchestra's inaugural course, also the programme for the three concerts. Janet Hilton would be soloist for Mozart's Clarinet Concerto. The 15 tutors would be drawn from RSAMD staff and from professional musicians then playing with Scottish ensembles, mainly SNO, SCO and BBCSSO. The winter concerts would be promoted as part of the SNO winter season. Of the applicants for the first course, Webb reported, 141 were from Strathclyde region, 65 from Lothian, 55 from Grampian, 41 from Tayside and so on, with one from the Western Isles, one from the Borders and none from Shetland. Equally noteworthy were those statistics which, year by year, were to be revealed during auditions, showing the remarkable pockets of strength in certain instruments and reflecting the quality of individual teachers or the musical commitment of certain schools. Nearly 400 young players had by then applied for places on the 1979 courses, all of them instrumentalists who had reached the required standard for audition, at least Grade VII – full justification, Webb argued, for giving Scotland its own national youth orchestra.

In many Scottish contexts, sensitivities are apparent, not least in relation to the English and England, which is some ten times greater in population than Scotland. Some Scots suffer from intimations of inferiority, many others from mere outrage, when notes of condescension are heard, or are thought to be heard, from south of the border. Such feelings were revealed from time to time during discussions and investigations leading up to the creation of NYOS. They were, too, aroused in relation to the recruitment of a conductor for the first winter course. It was announced in the press in December 1978 that a promising young newcomer, Simon Rattle, would be the conductor. For several weeks Rattle's agent proved awkwardly uncertain and eventually cancelled. Simon Rattle telephoned to apologise for the way his agent had treated NYOS. The later appointment of Edward Downes for the New Year concerts brought no hint of condescension on the part of either conductor or agent. Downes was no stranger to Scotland: in the late 1940s he had been the first full-time member of staff in the newly created department of music at Aberdeen University.

In the hope that the orchestra would be seen to be different from others, the council decided that the concert uniform would include grey trousers for male students and long grey skirts for female. Over the years the cost and availability of grey items of clothing were to present problems: eventually, after consultation with orchestra members, NYOS was to settle for the conventional black. Also the council agreed that regulations about haircuts should be less 'patronising and overbearing' than those imposed by NYOGB. Smoking and drinking were to be discouraged. It was also decided that, again distinct from NYOGB, all course members would take part in concerts, none finding themselves, with little warning, held backstage as reserves.

Once all auditions were completed, it was clear that the orchestra would rely markedly on a number of college students to ensure appropriate strength in some sections. At the inaugural concert, 28 students would come from the RSAMD, 7 from English colleges, 8 from St Mary's Music School; the average age was 17-plus; there were 69 girls and 45 boys. The budgeted costs for the first year were now almost £50,000, while the budgeted income in the spring of 1979 was £44,000. But optimism reigned. And Sir Alexander Gibson, whose promise of SNO administrative support had turned the tide at the critical meeting in June of 1977, was appointed honorary president.

A projected shortfall of £6,000 for the initial year of NYOS may, in retrospect, rate as a minor challenge. In fact a markedly optimistic disposition was required on the part of all concerned, bearing in mind, on the one hand, the excited expectations of a large number of young players and, on the other, the exposure to continued questioning and suspicion from many people in the world of music. Moreover, reliance on SNO administrative backup could not last for ever and the prospect of long-term funding was by no means secure. Bill Webb was already booking conductors, soloists, tutors and venues for future courses and concerts.

The chairman, Professor Pack, having assembled a widely representative council and mastered the legal technicalities of a new limited company, engaged himself in the laborious tasks of maintaining the goodwill and support of politicians, civil servants, councillors, people of influence in the arts, and – very importantly – the managers of trusts.

The first major grant had come from the Carnegie United Kingdom Trust whose friendly secretary, Geoffrey Lord, would eventually, in retirement, become a Council member. Lord had a talent for working along with applicants to help them meet Carnegie requirements. For the year 1979–80 Carnegie contributed £18,000.

With many trusts the applicant must exercise imagination and ingenuity in defining categories that will hopefully correspond with a trust's aims or with the personal preferences of trustees. So a list of good causes and essentials was devised by NYOS which included: bursaries for the less well off; conductors' and soloists' fees; hire or purchase of music and/or instruments; purchase of music stands; purchase of office equipment; purchase of recording equipment; mobility fund for travel expenses. A prolonged correspondence between Professor Pack and the Scottish International Education Trust resulted eventually in an annual £1,000 towards mobility. And in 1985 the SIET made a grant to enable NYOS to purchase a complete set of sturdy music stands.

Professor Pack had already negotiated at length with the Convention of Scottish Local Authorities. In the early years of NYOS he would have to cope with the ever-watchful Musicians' Union (MU), which fortunately presented fewer obstacles than Ruth Railton had encountered with the MU in founding and developing the NYOGB. In *Daring to Excel* she recalls that in the late 1940s she was accused by MU representatives of 'training up young people to take away our jobs'; also of setting out 'to show them up', this because the MU representatives noted that some of the young players were better than them.[1]

The main problem to be faced by NYOS with the MU would be that some of the senior NYOS members, by then in college, were already MU members and therefore were in a position to demand a fee if NYOS was being recorded or broadcast. Professor Pack met the MU's Scottish district organiser and argued that the students were signing up for educational courses with NYOS and that concerts were a part of that education. Recordings or broadcasts would be abandoned if full fees had to be paid. At this time the NYOGB did not admit music students from colleges; the European Community Youth Orchestra paid no fees for TV recordings. Tactfully and tactically, Professor Pack proposed that the MU be represented on NYOS Council. By 1982 the MU's Scottish district organiser served on NYOS Council as trades union representative for the Scottish Trades Union Congress. And the MU would make welcome donations to NYOS and NYJOS funds.

When Professor Pack had begun writing to the Scottish Arts Council in May of 1978 the SAC had not before then granted subsidy to musical activities specifically for young people, though the Arts Council of Great Britain was then funding the NYOGB to the extent of £20,000 per annum, and by 1979, £25,000. The SAC seemed willing to contribute to the commissioning of a new work for NYOS to play (over the years it would support the commissioning of quite a number) but was still hesitant through 1979 at the thought of funding amateur musicians. For NYOS it was argued that a number of professionals were to be employed as tutors. An approach was made by William Webb to the SAC's director of regional development: Webb pointed out that NYOS planned to hold courses and give concerts in as many centres as possible in Scotland. Eventually, by the spring of 1980, the SAC music committee was beginning to look favourably on NYOS, and the NYOS accounts for 1981 would show a grant from the SAC of £10,000.

Meantime Professor Pack approached the Scottish Education Department (SED), from which came a list of the conditions that would have to be met, including the presentation of audited accounts, this before there could be annual accounts to audit. Then in May from the SED came:

> Because of financial restrictions on government expenditure it will not be possible in the current financial year to make grant payments to bodies which have not hitherto been in receipt of them. We shall, however, keep you in mind for 1981–82.

The SED, later Scottish Office Education Department (SOED), would not, in fact, be contributing anything towards NYOS income until 1984, when it took over such funding from the SAC, by then at the level of £19,000.

In November of 1979, addressing a meeting of SAMA in Edinburgh, Professor Pack was able to report that the three main sources of money up to that point had been the Carnegie UK Trust, BP as sponsors, and those local authorities which had paid fees for orchestra members. Donations had also come from the Gannochy Trust, the Hinrichshen Foundation, Shell UK Ltd, J. R. Arthur Rank Group Charity, the Musicians' Union, the macRobert Trust, and the Scottish International Education Trust. 'I think,' Professor Pack said, 'we shall need to have additional support if we are to meet our commitments.' He was speaking three months after the first major NYOS commitment, the inaugural summer course for 113 young players. This had been held at Trinity College, Glenalmond, Perthshire, followed by three concerts – in Falkirk, Aberdeen and Dundee.

The first of these concerts may best be described as a singular event. It took place on Sunday, 12 August 1979 in a Big Top at Callendar Park, Falkirk, as part of the 1979 Falkirk Tryst which aimed to celebrate three centuries of gatherings at which (the local provost said in the concert programme) 'the culture and folklore of the Gael was heard in counterpoint with the sound of the traditional fiddles, Highland bagpipe and Lallans ballad'. To an occasion so described, the music of Mozart, Tchaikovsky and Respighi perhaps brought some degree of novelty. However, the programme began with Hamish McCunn's Overture, *The Land of the Mountain and the Flood*, for which performance the heavens opened and nearly flooded the huge tent. During the final item, Respighi's *Pines of Rome*, the rain eased sufficiently for the audience to hear the supportive cries of birds assembling above the tent.

The following evening NYOS, joining the International Festival of Youth Orchestras in Aberdeen's rain-proof Music Hall, gave what Malcolm Rayment of the Glasgow *Herald* described as the orchestra's first performance 'under good conditions'. He went on:

'Can a youth orchestra of real quality be built in a week? Before this concert I would have thought it impossible but, like everyone else present, I was staggered by what I heard.'[2]

The packed audience gave the new orchestra a standing ovation which lasted nearly ten minutes. Two days later the Dundee *Courier* reported that the first concert by NYOS in Dundee's Caird Hall had been delayed the previous night for more than a quarter of an hour as more than 300 latecomers sought tickets. Eventually around 1,400 warmly applauded the orchestra.

The *Guardian* critic, John Martin, said that NYOS had 'satisfied the highest hopes of its well wishers'.[3] Conrad Wilson, of *The Scotsman*, wrote, 'We shall certainly be hearing more of the National Youth Orchestra of Scotland.'[4] In Chapter Seven Conrad Wilson writes further about the NYOS.

TWO

Players

III

Band of Angels

At the BP press conference in January 1979, when he received the first cheque from BP for £6,000, Professor Pack said:

> The creation of the orchestra has in itself been an act of faith. The arrangement of courses and concerts has to proceed a long time ahead of the events, and when our first course and the concerts were being arranged last summer we had not even a penny of money that we could call our own.

It was a remarkable act of faith, justified primarily, and for some time solely, by Sir Alexander Gibson's offer of administrative support. Next, Carnegie came to the aid of the party. Then BP came to the rescue. And so, NYOS would get by with a little, sometimes a lot of, help from its friends – and much later its Friends. Mention can be made here of only a few of those many friends to whom NYOS has been indebted.

Sir John Drummond, who was director of the Edinburgh International Festival from 1979 to 1983, has written of those years: 'We were only at the beginning of the age of sponsorship'.[1] Drummond recalls that BP was in at that beginning: BP had been the first Festival sponsor, supporting a 'world-beating' *Carmen* production in 1977. Then in 1979, for the Festival, BP sponsored a Degas exhibition, and in 1980 the Australian Dance Theatre. NYOS, however, offered BP a novel opportunity: at the January 1979 press conference Mr Basil Butler, for BP, said this was the first time that his companies had had an opportunity of being in at the birth of a new organisation.

BP did the new baby proud: over a period of 16 years BP provided nearly a million pounds in guaranteed annual subventions. In addition it provided generous support of varying kinds, one of the most generous in 1983 when it funded the reconvening of NYOS 12 days after the conclusion of its summer course so that the orchestra could perform for the first time in the Edinburgh Festival, with Sir Alexander Gibson as conductor. This was Drummond's last Edinburgh Festival as director. To his great credit Drummond believed in supporting youth orchestras: 'I have a total enthusiasm for the excitement and energy that a good youth orchestra can generate with a fine conductor.' Drummond became the BBC's controller of music in 1985 and retired from his command of the Proms in 1995; twice in those years (in 1988 and 1993) NYOS played at the Proms: 'Such was my enthusiasm,' Drummond wrote, 'that in 1993 we actually had five (youth orchestras).'[2]

In May of 1980, Anthony J. Willcocks, director of BP's Public Affairs Scotland, wrote to Professor Pack confirming BP's revised intention, now to sponsor NYOS to the extent of £150,000 spread over five years, commencing in 1981. Professor Pack, worried about the recurring NYOS deficit, went at one stage to Edinburgh to talk personally to Willcocks and ask if a second sponsor might be sought. Willcocks said, 'No! We don't want a BP–Coca-Cola Orchestra' – which may explain the continuing level of BP generosity and also Item 1 in the sponsorship terms agreed in October of 1980 with Professor Pack:

> BP will be acknowledged as sponsors of the Orchestra. Contributions, donations and support may be sought from other organisations and individuals but no other organisation will be referred to as a 'sponsor of the Orchestra'. With the consent of BP other organisations will be permitted to sponsor individual concerts provided that the usual recognition of BP's role as the Orchestra's sponsor is unaffected. BP's consent will be considered in the context of any potential conflict of interests and will not be unreasonably withheld.

The Orchestra will have a logo including the BP shield and this will be used on all items of stationery including letterheads, labels, leaflets, posters, programmes, banners etc. BP will be responsible for all design costs in the use of the Orchestra's logo. Designs will be submitted by BP for the approval of the Council and once approved will not subsequently be changed without BP's consent.

Players in the Orchestra will wear ties or cravats incorporating the BP shield as already agreed by the Council and the design of these will not be changed without BP's consent.

So far as it is in their power, the Orchestra's administration will offer BP up to 5 per cent or 50 (whichever is greater) of the best available seats free of charge at each of the Orchestra's concerts. Seats above this number will be paid for by BP at normal commercial prices.

BP will be invited to nominate one representative for election to the Council of the NYOS and such election will not unreasonably be witheld.

In those early years BP helped to create a sound structure for NYOS finances. It also provided a second council member, in Geoffrey Phillips, a man of mature BP experience who was also richly informed in all matters musical. He attended many NYOS concerts and could be relied upon to provide an authentic 'Bravo' at the conclusion of a work, thus – perhaps in some remote island sports hall – offering appropriate supportive guidance for an audience unaccustomed to the ways of the urban concert hall. Geoffrey Phillips continued on NYOS council alongside Tony Willcocks' successors as BP external affairs co-ordinators, John A. E. Hughes and Ian M. T. Sandison.

In the very first NYOS programme, for the 1979 inaugural concerts in Falkirk, Aberdeen and Dundee, Mr Basil Butler, director of BP Petroleum Development, wrote a goodwill message which spoke of deeper reasons:

Perhaps I could take this opportunity to answer a question we are often asked: Why do we contribute to such events and organisations? Is it for the publicity, or are we trying to salve our conscience? I like to think the reasons go far deeper. BP has a long history in Scotland of which I think we can justly be proud. We are part of the economic fabric of the country, but we are also as much members of the community as anyone else. And as such we feel that we are bound to play our part in the social and cultural heritage of Scotland. If, in some small way, we can help to bring pleasure and enjoyment to people's lives, we believe that others too will be encouraged – each in their own way – to think of what they can contribute to society rather than, as seems to be so prevalent at the moment, what they can take out.

From the start, many guests of consequence were invited by BP to concerts and post-concert receptions. Other sponsors, not least the Bank of Scotland, sometimes equalled BP in this respect. Thus it was ensured that influential people in Scotland were made aware of NYOS' early achievements, also that NYOS, including its young players, would acquire that level of self-esteem which matters so much to people who are bringing a new organisation into existence.

NYOS had committed itself to reaching those parts of Scotland which no other large symphony orchestra had visited. Mr Willcocks wrote in the programme for the August 1980 NYOS Tour of the Highlands and Northern Isles:

It was our hope, in BP, that the Orchestra would be able to take its music the length and breadth of Scotland and the visit this summer to Shetland, Orkney and the Highlands is in part a fulfilment of that hope. The concert at Sullom Voe Terminal will, in fact, create for the Orchestra a record as the farthest point north at which a full symphony orchestra has played in the United Kingdom.

The orchestra had gathered at Strathallan School, in Perthshire, for a training session, then embarked on the MV *St Clair* at Aberdeen, BP banner flying, for the voyage to Lerwick. The NYOS brass section played into the small hours to the surprised delight of most passengers. The NYOS company totalled 140. BP joined with P&O Ferries Ltd to share the cost of the orchestra's journey to Lerwick. Accommodation was provided at the new Lerwick school hostel. On the Sunday morning, after breakfast, the orchestra buses set off for Sullom Voe, arriving in time for morning break in a hut where all manner of soft drinks, crisps, biscuits, chocolate bars etc., were laid out, courtesy of BP. 'Take all you want,' said Mr Willcocks. Orchestra members wanted a lot – and wanted for nothing.

They were then required to rehearse, after which they were led to a hut where a massive multi-course lunch was laid on. Then a smallish but select audience, mainly of BP personnel, gathered for an afternoon concert in the spacious Hilltop Centre, an entertainment venue more accustomed to music from such people as Shirley Bassey. Nicholas Kraemer, the conductor, courageously led the players through a creditable performance of Wagner's *Flying Dutchman* Overture, Elgar's *Enigma Variations*, Mozart's Oboe Concerto (soloist, an orchestra member, Elizabeth Fyfe) and Ravel's *Daphnis and Chloe*, Suite No. 2. Then the players were led to a canteen at which a rich and varied high tea was on offer. As Tony Willcocks rightly described it, 'a full symphony orchestra'. Also, as he had said, NYOS had now played at the farthest point north.

Mr Willcocks was so impressed with the brass section's impromptu performance on the MV *St Clair*, and on later occasions, that a NYOS Brass Quintet was recruited for an Easter Tour in 1981, visiting by helicopter the Forties Charlie Oil Platform and the MSV *Tharos*, also giving concerts in Dyce, Aberdeen and Patrington. Mr Willcocks was then responsible for BP's commissioning of *A Scots Folk Song Suite* by Alan Fernie, a trombonist in NYOS from 1979 till 1981. The suite was performed in the 1983 summer concerts and again at New Year 1984.

In the 1980 Tour of the Highlands and Northern Isles, the day after the Sullom Voe visit, the orchestra gave a concert for a local audience of over 500 in Anderson High School's new games hall. The next two concerts were in the Phoenix Cinema, Kirkwall. Getting from Lerwick to Kirkwall on time presented difficulties. The NYOS party of 140 had to wait – and be fed – in fog-bound Lerwick while plans were made for the company to travel, not by air as planned, but by rough sea overnight in the hurriedly chartered *Orcadia*, which was not designed or equipped for luxury travel. A bemused company of young players disembarked at 5 a.m., led by their conductor, Nicholas Kraemer, who suggested that they welcome the Orkney dawn by joining him in doing press-ups at the quayside.

NYOS was enormously lucky, after its initial and complicated birth pangs, not only to land a major sponsor so generous as BP but also, for a number of years, to be given so much free hospitality from the then amply funded Highland and Island authorities: on the 1980 tour all hostel accommodation in Lerwick and Kirkwall was provided free by the Islands councils' education departments. This made it possible for NYOS to fulfil, at an early stage, its aim to perform in places unfamiliar with symphony orchestras. Sometimes such an audience is especially appreciative. Live performances can be much more interesting than a broadcast: 'live performance is the oxygen of art'.[3]

The programme for the 1980 tour, which also included Thurso and Inverness, listed 17 sources of funding. By 2002 the number of sponsors and donors requiring to be thanked in the printed programme was nearly 200, not counting over 160 Friends. In the past 25 years, hundreds of companies, institutions, trusts, councils and individuals have contributed in one way or another to the funding of NYOS. It was, of course, to be a matter for regret on NYOS' part that BP eventually, in 1995, took its sponsorship elsewhere, though this was after a longer period of generous funding than is normally expected of any sponsor. While it lasted, BP sponsorship was all that a new youth orchestra could ask for – and more. In the course of its association with NYOS, BP sponsorship was deservedly recognised in a series of awards from, and administered by, the Association for Business Sponsorship of the Arts.

In the 1985 New Year programme John Hughes, of BP, in confirming BP's then commitment to NYOS, wrote:

> That NYOS is now an established part of Scotland's cultural activities is indisputable, and I am glad that other leading representatives of the commercial and industrial life of the community are now coming forward to identify themselves with the orchestra's performances, both at home and abroad. I hope that the trend will continue and gather pace: this will be the best way of securing the future prosperity and success of NYOS.

In fact, BP set an example that is not likely to be matched.

BAND OF ANGELS

For all that NYOS has received, its staff and council have been truly thankful. They have laboured, often strained, to ensure that benefactors were glad to have supported the making of music by the young. Sponsors, donors and government-funding bodies all want to know that their money is well spent. How does one best impress them? How to ensure appropriate prestige and quality? Quality in the arts may be at variance with popularity or familiarity. One Scottish education minister, not a regular concert goer, exclaimed at a post-concert reception that the evening had been much too heavy for him. Would he have been better pleased had he already been familiar with the name of the conductor or of the soloist? But famous conductors and soloists may be rather expensive (so far no NYOS conductor has been individually sponsored). Some conductors do not welcome the idea of touring with a young orchestra. They may wish only to pick up for final rehearsal from a training conductor. But extended contact with one good conductor is valuable for a youth orchestra.

Some distinguished conductors may not be especially good with youth orchestras. Lady Beecham wouldn't allow her husband Sir Thomas to conduct a youth orchestra: 'She thought it *infra dig* for him to conduct kids'.[4] On the other hand, Zubin Mehta, like many other eminent conductors, enjoys the association: 'The thing about youth orchestras is they just don't know how dangerous it is. They give everything all the time.'[5] Junichi Hirokami, who has conducted NYOS three times, is quoted in a NYOS programme: 'They always make me feel younger. They absorb my energy, they fill me with the spirit of music, which is something I, as a professional musician, thought I had forgotten ten years ago. That inspires me.'

In 1988, on NYOS' second visit to Holland, James Loughran, who has also conducted NYOS three times, was interviewed by a Dutch journalist. In an article headed '*Spelen met jonge musici verfrissend*' ('Playing with young musicians is refreshing') Loughran was reported: 'Every conductor should be obliged to work with young folk once a year. It is very refreshing. It prevents fossilisation [. . .] They are itching to play something fine. They are not yet jaded, they think positively.'[6]

So conductors must be found who like – or are allowed, by spouses or agents – to work with young people and who also, with the aid of good instrumental tutors, are likely to get the best out of the orchestra.

45

(Nicholas Braithwaite, who conducted NYOS six times, from its inaugural concerts in 1979 until the New Year concerts in 1987, found a wife in the NYOS strings – he married violinist Gillian Haggarty, who was in NYOS from 1980 till 1985.)

The comparatively long rehearsal time required for youth orchestras can make them popular with a young conductor wishing to add a new major work to his or her repertoire. Will the press critics detect and appreciate the fresh approach? The conductor for the Highlands and Islands tour in 1980 was Nicholas Kraemer who had till then worked mainly with chamber and operatic ensembles. Conrad Wilson, who accompanied NYOS on this tour, wrote: 'his [Kraemer's] feeling for line was rewardingly in evidence, but responsive also to the larger, more lustrous washes of sound untacked in Ravel's second *Daphnis and Chloe* Suite, played with impressive command of the swirling rhythm of the finale'.[7]

One girl percussion player said of Kraemer's conducting of *Daphnis and Chloe*: 'Every time we come to the end of the Ravel I want to throw back my head and laugh and laugh'.[8]

By the summer of 2003, NYOS will have had 27 conductors, 10 of them conducting the orchestra more than once, and NYOS will have played along with 52 soloists, with 5 of them more than once. Inevitably the quality and the chemistry are unpredictable, as are the critics who review the concerts. 'The past few years have proved erratic for the orchestra,' said a *Scotsman* reviewer in July 2002, suggesting that much depended on who was on the rostrum.[9]

Youth orchestras vary in personnel and in strength from one year to the next. Over a few years a group of players can develop orchestral competence and confident cohesion which any guest conductor will – along with audience and press critics – recognise and welcome. In the summer of 1982 Nicholas Braithwaite, conducting NYOS for the third time, took the orchestra on the long Viking Tour with Christine Cairns and Nigel Kennedy as soloists (Kennedy had been soloist 18 months previously on the 1980–81 winter course conducted by Norman Del Mar). When the orchestra was together in Denmark at the end of the very successful Viking Tour, Braithwaite raised a timely alarm: he had worked since 1979 with a group of strong players many of whom, he now realised, would not be with NYOS the following year when the orchestra was to appear for the first time at the Edinburgh Festival. For this, an impressive performance was necessary and BP was to be providing generous extra funding.

From the original orchestra of 1979, 32 remained till 1982: only 9 of those would be in the 1983 NYOS. Of the 123 players in the 1983 summer course, only 47 (38 per cent) had been on the 1982 Viking Tour. Fortunately, Christopher Adey, who had gained a reputation as a strong training conductor, was recruited to take the 1983 summer orchestra through its course in Stornoway, performing twice there and then in Inverness, Pitlochry and Aberdeen. NYOS reconvened 12 days later for the Festival event, with Sir Alexander Gibson conducting and Isobel Buchanan, soprano, as soloist. The performance, concluding with the demanding Nielsen Symphony No. 4, *The Inextinguishable*, won prolonged applause from a packed and enthusiastic Usher Hall audience, as well as critical acclaim from the press.

Then as before the tutorial staff, under the leadership of Peter Mountain and Edgar Williams, deserved a great deal of the credit. Neither audience, nor critics, nor sponsors can be expected to appreciate the degree of credit due to the tutors, or indeed to those who have, along with the director, laboriously conducted the auditions. The processes of audition and tutoring constitute a principal distinguishing feature of youth orchestras such as NYOS. Fortunately, first Harrison's (Clyde) in the early '90s and then the Royal Bank of Scotland provided sponsorship for auditions, a costly element in NYOS finances. Standard Life sponsorship, announced in September 2002, as in the earlier sponsorship by Hydro-Electric, included sponsorship of NCOS auditions.

South of the Border, a distinguishing feature of the early years of the National Youth Orchestra of Great Britain had been its policy of engaging remarkably young players as soloists. The soloist for the first NYOGB course, in 1948, playing Mozart's Piano Concerto in A K488, was a 13 year old, Elizabeth Powell. In 1954 for the NYOGB's fourth appearance at the Edinburgh Festival the soloist was 11-year-old Allan Schiller (Mozart's Piano Concerto in G K453). Wendy Waterman was only nine when she was soloist in 1955 (Bach Klavier Concerto in D minor). Stephanie Bamford was ten in January 1957 (Mozart Piano Concerto in D K537). It was NYOGB policy to engage young soloists.

NURTURING TALENT

Under the NYOGB constitution at that time a professional soloist could not be employed.[10]

NYOS policy on soloists varied in the early years. The soloist for the first NYOS concerts in 1979 was a professional, Janet Hilton, then principal clarinet of the Scottish Chamber Orchestra. For the 1980 summer concerts, one of the two soloists was Elizabeth Fyfe, a founder member of the orchestra (Mozart Oboe Concerto in C major K314). In August 1981 two orchestra members, John Grant and Saida de Lyon, were joint soloists in Mozart's Flute and Harp Concerto K299. They played in what was one of the most awkward venues NYOS has experienced: the first of the three concerts on that tour was in the Academy Hall, Dumfries, where the large orchestra almost filled the downstairs area and most of the small audience had to settle for being perched in the balcony from which they could see only part of the orchestra. Pamela Redman, violin, and Susan Young, viola, were the soloists for Mozart's Sinfonia Concertante K364 in January 1982; this was the one occasion on which NYOS has played in Edinburgh's Playhouse. The 1982 tour also included concerts in the Ayr Pavilion and Glasgow's City Hall, all with Sir Alexander Gibson conducting.

In the summer of 1984 NYOS gave six concerts, one of them by the NYOS wind ensemble, playing in Westray Community Centre. (This exercise was made possible by a donation from Occidental Oil Inc: sponsors are more readily found for small one-off projects). At the other 1984 concerts, in Kirkwall, Thurso, Inverness and Aberdeen, the soloists were orchestra members. Claire Docherty, violin (Ravel *Tzigane*), who was with NYOS from 1979 until 1985 and Christopher Bradley, trumpet (Aruturian Trumpet Concerto in A♭ major). Since then all NYOS soloists have been professionals, some of them comparatively young. Through those years of experiment BP was consistently supportive, not least in promoting the efforts, first of the brass section, then of Alan Fernie for his Scots Folk Song Suite.

Three former NYOS members were to be invited to return as professionals, two as soloist and one as conductor. Evelyn Glennie was a member of the NYOS percussion team from the summer of 1981 till the summer of 1982. Thirty years earlier, John Dalby had begun to make north-east Scotland a focus of specialism in percussion and over the years had done much to raise percussion from being what he called 'the Cinderella of the orchestral world'.[11] Evelyn Glennie was a beneficiary of the local specialism. In the early 1980s she was striving to persuade those in charge of such matters that her deafness should be no impediment to her pursuing a career in percussion. She writes: 'a brief concert tour in Scotland with the National Youth Orchestra of Scotland early in January helped to keep up my spirits'.[12] In spite of some strong opposition she was accepted by the Royal Academy of Music in London. In the summer of 1982 she was on the Viking Tour:

> The Scottish composer John McLeod accompanied us, conducting his tone poem *The Gokstad Ship*. He has since then become a good friend and has composed a number of percussion pieces that are important items in my repertoire, including his Percussion Concerto and *The Song of Dionysius* which I played at my solo Prom debut in July 1989.[13]

Evelyn Glennie was soloist with NYOS in the summer of 1987 and at New Year 1988 (premiere of John McLeod's Percussion Concerto, written for Evelyn Glennie), then at New Year 1992 (Jolivet, Percussion Concerto), and in the summer of 1995 (Heath, African Sunrise–Manhattan Rave). The Heath work and Glennie's performances of it were sponsored by Hydro-Electric: the Scottish Arts Council subsidised the commissioning of the work, as over the years it has supported the commissioning of many new works performed by NYOS.

Colin Currie, who was in the percussion section of NYOS from 1990 to 1994, has been booked as soloist with NYOS for the 2005 New Year concerts. When he was 15, Currie won the Gold Medal of the Shell/London Symphony Orchestra Music Scholarship. In 1994 he became the first percussion finalist in the BBC Young Musician of the Year competition. In 2001 he was awarded the Royal Philharmonic Society's Young Artist Award for his outstanding contribution to innovative music-making in the year 2000. He continually commissions and performs new works and has worked with orchestras in the UK, the Continent and the States.

Garry Walker, a NYOS cellist from 1980 to 1982, also a member of Camerata Scotland, and winner of the 1999 Leeds Conductors'

Competition, returned to NYOS as conductor of Prokofiev's *Romeo and Juliet* in the New Year 2000 Concerts. He was sole conductor for the 2002 New Year Concerts.

> The 26-year-old Edinburgh-born maestro – making his first full-concert appearance with NYOS was magnificent in the Mahler (Symphony No. 1) making the most of the dramatic twists and turns, but most importantly, welding its filigree components into a logical and combustible structure. Clarity was paramount.[14]

Garry Walker conducted Camerata Scotland in the Spring of 2003 and will join Colin Currie in the 2005 New Year concerts.

These New Year concerts were the last of the New Year concerts sponsored by Bank of Scotland, which also sponsored the National Youth Jazz Orchestra of Scotland for five years of NYJOS' early development. At a Bank of Scotland post-concert reception in Edinburgh's Sheraton Hotel in the 1980s, Professor Pack, NYOS chairman, had expressed the hope that the Bank might be a Friend for Life. The Bank's sponsorship of no fewer than 20 New Year concerts represented a life longer in years than any other sponsorship NYOS has enjoyed.

The Bank of Scotland's support of New Year concerts in Edinburgh overlapped for 16 years with Radio Clyde's sponsorship of the NYOS New Year concerts in Glasgow, beginning in 1981. Radio Clyde also commissioned John McLeod's *The Gokstad Ship* in 1982.

From 1993 till 2000 LASMO Arts Trust sponsored the Staffa Music Awards. These were based on the audition performances of senior candidates nominated by eight of the UK's leading music colleges. On the night of the Staffa award concert the finalists have aimed to please an adjudication panel as well as the audience. In 1998 the LASMO Arts Trust decided to augment the music award to incorporate a separate category for singers. The first of the finals for the Staffa competition was held at Haddo House and the last under LASMO sponsorship was in Fyvie Castle. Others were in the Queen's Hall, Edinburgh, and in the RSAMD Glasgow. In both Edinburgh and Glasgow the competitions were accompanied by performances from Camerata Scotland, of which LASMO was the principal sponsor from 1996 till 2001. From 2002, NYOS itself sponsored the NYOS Staffa Awards.

BAND OF ANGELS

In April 1996 the John Lewis Partnership began its support of Camerata Scotland with a series of three John Lewis Partnership-promoted concerts: these were in St Giles' Cathedral, Edinburgh; St Michael's Parish Church, Linlithgow; and St Mary's Parish Church, Haddington. The support was repeated in 1999 with three concerts, two in Greyfriars Church, Edinburgh, one in St Mary's, Haddington, and one in Dunfermline Abbey. The abbey concert was partnered with an afternoon children's concert for Fife council.

Camerata Scotland has been engaged in concerts along with Staffa Awards and, since 2001, with the National Children's Orchestra of Scotland. Hydro-Electric sponsored NCOS from its inception until 2001: then in September 2002 Standard Life announced its sponsorship of NCOS, committing itself to support the work of NCOS, including auditions, residential training and public performances for the following three years.

At the 2001 Spring Concert in the Glasgow Royal Concert Hall four members of the orchestra played in Bach's Concerto for Four Pianos. The concert, attended by the Earl and Countess of Wessex, was sponsored by Stirling Shipping. Camerata Scotland took over for the second half of the evening.

Hydro-Electric had also been sponsor of the 1995 NYOS summer tour, for which the concert venues included Kirkwall, Thurso, Fort William, Glasgow, Elgin and Aberdeen. Its sponsorship of NYOS ended after its merger with Southern Electric. The merger or take-over of a firm is liable to result in a cutting-back, often the termination – always the reviewing – of sponsorship or funding, as happened with several of the companies mentioned above.

Continuing contact with previous and potential sponsors can become rewarding when a company wishes to focus attention on a noteworthy event or anniversary in the company's history. ScotRail, a generous sponsor in the 1980s and early 1990s, marked the inaugural concert of NYOS Chamber Orchestra (later Camerata Scotland) in 1992 by funding the commissioning of Edward McGuire's *Symphonies of Trains*, to commemorate the 150th anniversary of the opening of the Edinburgh and Glasgow Railway. Then in 1994 ScotRail sponsored the orchestra's concert in Fort William, celebrating 100 Years of the West Highland Line. If PR personnel really want to provide sponsorship they are the most likely people to think up good reasons for a one-off project, especially if it is associated with the history of the firm or society. In 2002 the Royal Scottish Geographical Society supported the commissioning of Gordon McPherson's 'South' which marked the centenary of the Voyage of the Scotia, the Scottish National Antarctic Expedition, a 33,000-mile voyage of discovery.

Sponsors' reasons, short- and long-term, are various and, as Basil Butler suggested above, sometimes deep. Attitudes and personnel keep changing. So the pursuit of funding has to be painstaking and indefatigable (see Chapter Eight).

IV

Home and Abroad

In March of 1979 William Webb suggested to NYOS Council that the 1980 summer course might be held on a ship. In June of 1979 he reported that he had visited the Central Bureau of Educational Visits and Exchanges where two possible areas for an overseas tour had been recommended, namely Scandinavia and Israel. The National Youth Orchestra of Great Britain had visited Israel 14 years previously; the County of Essex Youth Orchestra had gone there in 1978. NYOS could be accommodated in a kibbutz: as Israel owed Great Britain a large number of nights of accommodation NYOS could probably be accommodated for a whole course free of charge. There were many excellent concert halls in Israel and there would be little travelling once NYOS reached Israel, since the three main centres, Jerusalem, Tel-Aviv and Haifa, were all comparatively close together.

William Webb also told the council he was confident that NYOS would be welcome in Finland. The British Council might make a guarantee against loss up to a pre-agreed maximum for a foreign tour, provided the British Council had an interest in promoting concerts by British artists in the country concerned. An application including Finland would be sympathetically considered; the orchestra's programme would have to include at least one work by a twentieth-century British composer. Mr Webb tabled a draft schedule for a tour which might include Helsinki and Turku. Then he suggested that Leningrad (St Petersburg) might also be considered, since it was so close to Helsinki.

Eleven years later, planning began for a NYOS tour in 1991 in the south of what had been the Soviet Union, in Georgia, where it was proposed that NYOS should give a concert tour. The Georgian State Symphony Orchestra was booked to visit Scotland in April 1991; the Georgia Centre for Music and Culture offered NYOS accommodation, travel and a daily allowance whilst in Georgia. After rehearsals in Tbilisi, NYOS would give concerts in Tbilisi and in the Black Sea resort of Pitsunda. The estimated cost of air charter would be over £60,000. A Soviet conductor, Sergei Vlasov, was booked for the tour.

Some of the best-laid touring schemes *gang aft a-gley*. No NYOS course has so far been held on a ship. NYOS has never made it to Israel, Finland, Leningrad, Tbilisi or Pitsunda. In 1991 Gulf War politics made a NYOS visit to Georgia unwise. Sergei Vlasov did conduct the 1991 concerts but the farthest east NYOS got that year was Paris. Tragically, several years later Sergei Vlasov was killed, having by chance become involved in a feud between criminals in Russia. Troubles in Israel and thereabouts from the 1980s onwards would preclude any possibility of a course and concerts there. In 2002 signs of political and economic instability in South America resulted in the cancellation of plans for a tour there by Camerata Scotland.

Countless possibilities and promises – for concert venues and orchestra accommodation, as for conductors and soloists – are exhaustively explored and costed. Some materialise. The British Council can be very helpful: much may depend on the personnel who happen currently to be in the countries concerned. Personnel keep changing.

In 1979 when William Webb was looking ambitiously beyond Scotland on NYOS' behalf, the council decided that NYOS should not go abroad before 1982 because it was committed to showing the orchestra's flag in Scotland first. Indeed, partly for tactical reasons in preliminary negotiations with local councils and other funding bodies, the promise had been made that NYOS would aim to take its large symphony orchestra where others had till then not reached. This would always prove difficult: other large orchestras had been prevented from visiting comparatively small communities not only because of the limited hall space, nor because of the financial challenge of ensuring adequate box office returns or local subsidy, but also because of inadequate or inappropriate staging, and sometimes because access was impossible for harps and percussion equipment. The provision of new sports halls eased the problems of space and access though not always of audience size. Or of acoustics. On NYOS' first visit to Fort William the summer heat made necessary the opening of the hall windows but seemed also to have given singular zest to the cries of the local seagulls who contributed markedly alien harmonies, especially to Vaughan Williams' *London Symphony.*

Winter can make access to many areas of Scotland uncertain, while summer, if tourism is at its peak, can make accommodation impossible in the locality. University and college hostels may be making good money from conferences in the summer, and in the winter they have difficulty in holding staff over Christmas and New Year. So NYOS players, in order to play in certain concert venues, may have to travel two or three hours by coach from and to their course headquarters. The planning and the financing of a concert tour in Scotland may present as many administrative difficulties, in advance and on the spot, as for a foreign tour. The prospect of ample and relaxed accommodation, along with convenient and appropriate concert venues, would have eased many difficulties for NYOS over the past 25 years. A serious blow came when it was announced that the one eminently suitable site, St Andrew's Campus, Bearsden, which served NYOS well for 13 years, would no longer be available; this required the director to consider looking south of the border for a new training base.

Though NYOS did not go outside Scotland until 1982, it went most pleasurably off the mainland in 1980 to Orkney and Shetland, both of these newly equipped with excellent school hostel accommodation, less spartan than was then available in Glenalmond or Strathallan for training courses. So in 1982 NYOS was very glad to have its training course, as well as two concerts, in Orkney. In 1983 it held its course and gave two concerts in Stornoway where again the modern hostel provision was enjoyed, but alas it is no longer available. NYOS was back in Kirkwall in 1984 ('at the very generous invitation of Orkney Islands Council', said the NYOS annual report in 1985). That was the year

Nurturing Talent

NYOS took a small woodwind, brass and percussion ensemble to the community centre on Westray. In summer 1986 NYOS was in Lerwick, this time performing in Shetland's new and spacious Clickimin Centre. 1987 saw a return to Stornoway and in 1989, 1995 and 2002 to Kirkwall, where in 2002 the orchestra performed in the new Pickaquoy Centre. The Kirkwall accommodation is now the best and most appropriate in Scotland for residential orchestral rehearsal periods.

Such visits to the island authorities inevitably depend to a great extent not only on the potential concert audiences but also on the local authorities' eagerness – expressed in generous financial terms – to house the large orchestra. In 1980 and 1982 the process was especially well oiled by oil: such financial lubrication had virtually disappeared by the end of the century. At the same time, the introduction of new regulations relating to the safety of juveniles has added to the difficulties of island visits.

Meantime, within the Scottish mainland, in addition to many performances in Glasgow, Edinburgh and Aberdeen (many appearances there to join in the International Youth Festival) NYOS has taken its hundred-plus players to Dundee, Inverness, Thurso, Perth, Dumfries, Ayr, Pitlochry, Stirling, Fort William, Elgin and Stranraer.

Though NYOS was on its first foreign tour in 1982, it didn't perform in England until 1988 when it gave its first BBC London Promenade Concert in the Albert Hall. Its next visit south of the border was in 1991 to Liverpool on its way to France. In 1993 NYOS paid its first of several successful visits to Birmingham Symphony Hall. In 1986 it played in Nottingham's Royal Concert Hall, and in 1999 it returned to Liverpool, in that year also making its first visit to Kendal.

In the 1970s there were still many young people in Scotland who had never been abroad, some not furth of mainland Scotland. For many schools and colleges in the 1960s and '70s there was – and still is – an undeniable cachet, a corporate ego-trip and a lot of individual pleasure, in undertaking a foreign tour. In those decades some school parties joined in education cruises that went to the Baltic and elsewhere. The travel experience, however, can sometimes be bruising, physically so if the economics of the exercise involve uncomfortable accommodation, say in ill-heated rooms or school halls, perhaps in shabby hostels or hotels equipped with shoddy bedding. The nadir for NYOS was reached in one European establishment where paper sheets combined with layers of dust on bare floors to make sleeping a distasteful experience. The food was awful, too. Never again.

A number of youth orchestras, under the fashionable compulsion to travel, have slept badly, eaten poorly and then, as a result, played badly to almost non-existent foreign audiences. Poor audiences are always more cheaply and comfortably available at home.

But there are good reasons for moving a youth orchestra around. At an early NYOS council meeting, Dr David Lumsden, then principal of the RSAMD, said that performing in front of a large audience was an essential part of the general training which NYOS should be able to offer. NYOS offered it from the start, in a variety of settings. Professor Pack wrote, in the programme for the 1983 New Year concerts:

> An orchestra aspiring to a high international reputation must undertake foreign tours from time to time in order to demonstrate its prowess to new audiences and submit itself to wider judgment. [. . .] After the orchestra had performed in no less than 13 towns and cities in Scotland it was time to demonstrate abroad the degree of excellence that is being achieved by Scotland's musical youth.

NYOS has been able to submit itself – successfully – to that wider judgment on many occasions. Before many enthusiastically appreciative audiences abroad it has shown what it can achieve. The benefit has been mutual. To draw and then please a packed Concertgebouw audience in Amsterdam; to charm a festive crowd in Tivoli Gardens, Copenhagen; to join with a local choir in the Nordland Musikkfestuke for a moving performance of Berlioz' *Requiem* in Bodø Cathedral, Norway; or, as part of the Berlin Festival, to win rapturous applause from a packed Konzerthaus – such occasions, rich in the shared experience of great music, help young players and their audiences to reach across many boundaries.

It is also good for young players to be required to please the smallest audiences: no one purchases a ticket eager to sit in an almost empty auditorium, so the performance should be made especially rewarding. For the first NYOS visit to Norway in 1982 the BBC, making a film of the tour, worked with the local TV company to record one concert, in a large hall, for which the audience totalled little more than a hundred. Norwegian music-lovers tend to migrate to holiday homes in the summer. So the audience was re-seated close to the platform, in an appropriate wedge formation so that a camera could, though with great care, track back and fore in front of the tightly packed group, thus giving the – somewhat boring – impression that the audience was adequate.

In its first 25 years NYOS symphony orchestra has gone abroad 11 times. It has visited Sweden, Denmark and Luxembourg once, the Faroe Islands twice, Germany twice, Norway three times and Holland seven times. Tom Odems, director of the Casino Theater, s'Hertogenbosch, Holland, who happened to own property in Crieff, was responsible for NYOS first being invited, in 1985, to Holland, where both NYOS and Camerata Scotland were to perform a number of times – NYOS being the first Scottish orchestra of any kind to have played in the Concertgebouw main hall. Again thanks to Tom Odems, plans were initiated in 2002 for NYJOS to perform abroad during the summer of 2003.

In 1985 NYOS had been booked to perform in Ripon Cathedral, as part of the Harrogate International Festival, on its way back to Scotland from a demanding tour in Holland, Belgium, Germany and Luxembourg – the orchestra's contribution to European Music Year 1985. The tour was, as the next annual report said, 'dogged by bad luck'. Two of the concerts abroad had to be cancelled, one because a North Sea Ferry ran aground whilst avoiding collision with another vessel, so the NYOS course was set back a day. The proposed concert in the Roman Amphitheatre in Trier was rained off. Then – all this on the orchestra's 13th course – a virus infection attacked the young players so severely that the Ripon concert had to be cancelled. The players managed to recover sufficiently from the disabling bug to fulfil their last engagement for that summer, in the Albert Hall, Stirling.

The 1985 summer course was unique in that the training course took place abroad, complete with 14 tutors, who accompanied the players via Hull by ferry to Rotterdam, then to Ochenburgh Centre, near the Hague. There the tutors were engaged in three sessions of instruction totalling seven hours, after which they were taken by coach to Schiphol Airport, Amsterdam, thence by air to Glasgow. That was a costly summer tour, in fact the total expenditure for that year was the highest NYOS had till then sustained.

Like armies, orchestras, not least youth orchestras, may be said to march – and also play – on their stomachs, though the expression would have been thought indelicate in Ripon in 1985. The planning of meals in transit and abroad can be difficult, even sensitive: the generous provision of what others see as local delights may not be received with the appropriate, far less appreciative, courtesies by nervous young guests at a foreign table. When NYOS first ventured abroad it landed at Torshavn and on arrival found the food of the Faroes, provided in the very comfortable hostel, was of a staple if uninspiring kind, markedly generous in muesli and yoghurt. Then one meal, specially provided in a local restaurant, was intended to introduce the players to items beloved of the natives. This array of delicacies met with something more than suspicion. Consumption of Faroese delicacies was made easier for a party of NYOS adults who were invited to a late-night event: so that they could tackle tit-bits of dried mutton and unidentifiable seafoods, they were encouraged to follow a local practice of washing such items down with strong local spirits.

The situation was different in Bodo ten years later when orchestra members were puzzled to the point of outrage because the health-conscious hotel chef never served pudding at meal-times. Eventually, after one concert, a pudding – ice cream – was served, upon seeing which the entire orchestra rose to its feet and sang the 'Hallelujah' chorus. The hotel staff liked the joke.

In August 1993, members of the new 37-strong Chamber Orchestra of NYOS (by 1996 retitled Camerata Scotland) were on tour in Japan where, according to the NYOS 1994 programme, 'they enjoyed many social functions and gatherings and were happy to experience a splendid menu of varied Japanese foods'. No complaints recorded. On this tour, Camerata Scotland took part in the opening concert, in Nagoya, of the World Youth Orchestra Festival; further performances, to packed and appreciative audiences, were given in Toyohashi, Ohta and Ichikawa.

The logistics of NYOS courses – reception, accommodation, movement by land, sea or air – call for a range of talents and qualities in the staff recruited to provide pastoral care. Previous useful experience of personnel in NYOS house staff has varied from command of a touring

Gigantisk « Requiem »

NYOS went to Bodø, Norway in 1992 to take part in the Nordland Musikkfestuke for a performance of Berlioz's *Requiem* in Bodø Cathedral with the local choir. The symphony orchestra was praised for a 'gigantic' experience that went 'far beyond the musical' and 'perhaps registered on seismographs throughout Scandinavia'.

Honderdtien toptalenten
Schots jeugdorkest muzikaal hoogtepunt

Schots toporkest in Schouwburg Casino

In Holland in 1998 NYOS won headlines, '110 Top Talents. Scottish Youth Orchestra musical high point'; and 'Scottish Top Orchestra in Casino Theatre'.

In Japan in 1993, the newly formed NYOS Chamber Orchestra (now Camerata Scotland) visited Japan to take part in the World Youth Orchestra Festival. The photograph shows the orchestra in rehearsal on a platform above which a banner reads, '57th Regular Toyo Symphony Orchestra International Exchange Concert'. The character for 'exchange' also translates as 'friendship'.

rugby team to supervision of a pre-school playgroup. The director has ultimate say in all matters when NYOS is on tour but he must rely in large measure on the house staff, who have oversight of morale and morals and much else. The morale of young players who have never previously been away from family (a situation now more common in NCOS than in NYOS) is usually easier to cope with than the behaviour of some older NYOS players who may have difficulty in holding to rules that must inevitably be imposed affecting drink, drugs or relations with the opposite sex. Comparatively few difficulties in these categories arose during training courses in the years when St Andrew's Campus Bearsden was in regular use. The college had a licensed bar, so there was no furtive dashing out by a daring group to test the resources of a local pub. Staff and all of the students could mix for refreshments and chat in the few evening hours of relaxation.

Bearing in mind the many hundreds of young players who have taken part in NYOS courses it is greatly to the credit of the staff, as it is to that of the players, that only a very few students have been required to leave during a course. No player can think him or herself indispensible. The morale of the whole company is damaged, however, if there is a vacant chair, if a player (after contact with parents) has been quickly sent home on the next available train or plane.

As for the staff, NYOS has been lucky to have been well served over the years by so many men and women of resilience and good humour. The duties of house staff are most exacting when the orchestra has to move from place to place, occasionally in crowded accommodation, sometimes with tiresome travel. Journeys by sea are sometimes a delight, sometimes not. Travel by air is not as novel for young people now as it was in the early 1980s. The movement of large instruments and equipment has been in the strong hands of always reliable transport staff, some of whom have come back year after year, intrigued by the variety of locations offered by NYOS tours. In the early years, as many as twelve staff were recruited for NYOS summer courses; in recent years eight or nine have sufficed, but for NCOS at least twelve support staff have been necessary. NCOS has been invited by the Chinese government to send a group of players to take part in a Children's Festival in Beijing in August of 2004. For this venture some 20 students, aged 8 to 14, will be accompanied by at least 10 NCOS staff.

NURTURING TALENT

While Camerata Scotland has travelled widely, the planning and management of a Camerata Scotland tour – for which no separate house staff are employed – are less exacting than for the 120-strong NYOS symphony orchestra. However, the 1997 exchange project with Camerata Australia, marking the 50th anniversary of the British Council in Australia, rated, in one reviewer's words, as 'not an undaunting manoeuvre'. The Scots welcomed a glimpse into daily Aussie life: in one centre they enjoyed the warm hospitality of host families who 'did much to challenge my soap opera-fed stereotypes' (Harriet Davidson writing in the 1998 New Year Programme). This exchange tour also involved the Scots players in welcoming their Australian counterparts to the UK, including some standard – maybe stereotyped – sight-seeing in 'Olde England' alongside performances in Birmingham, Manchester, and London (Barbican).

In August, 1998 Camerata Scotland venues included Reims Champagne Congrès, France; St Mary-in-the-Castle, Hastings; and St James's, Piccadilly. For Camerata Scotland the sizes of venue platforms present fewer problems than for the NYOS symphony orchestra so a greater number of performances in Scotland outside the main cities have been possible -- for example, in Kelso, Campbeltown, Glenrothes, Linlithgow, Haddington, Wick, Dunfermline, Stranraer, Arbroath, and Oban.

New opportunities for NYOS students began in the 1990s when arrangements were made for individual students to visit and perform with youth orchestras abroad. James Cheek was invited to play cor anglais and oboe, and Jenny Cooper to play bassoon, in the 80-strong Commonwealth Youth Orchestra which was held in conjunction with the 1998 Commonwealth Games in Malaysia. Also in the summer of 1998, Katie Duffy went to Spain to join as a first violin in a three-week orchestral course in Seville with the Joven Orquestra Nacional de Espana (a course which was free for its Spanish students, all their travel costs being paid). Concerts were in Pilas, Madrid and Lisbon. The following year Ruth E. Lunny joined with the same youth orchestra for a tour that included concerts in France and Luxembourg. In 2002 four NYOS violinists joined this orchestra. Altogether NYOS has arranged for NYOS symphony orchestra students to perform with orchestras abroad in Japan, USA, Australia, Spain, Italy, Austria, Malaysia and

Belgium. In turn, NYOS symphony orchestra has welcomed 24 visiting players from 15 countries, while Camerata Scotland has been host to players from England, Germany, Chile and Ireland.

These developments in international exchange have coincided with, and sometimes resulted from, the establishing of formal contacts by NYOS with orchestral and youth organisations abroad. In the spring of 1991 Richard Chester, NYOS director, visited Japan to become a member of the founding committee of the 1993 World Youth Orchestra Conference. He was on the committee of the 1993 World Youth Orchestra Festival in Nagoya, Japan. Since 1993 Chester has represented NYOS in the European Federation of National Youth Orchestras, of which he is now president; and he is a director of the World Federation of Amateur Orchestras which was founded in 1998.

V

Other Musical Ensembles

In the first Report and Accounts of the National Youth Orchestra of Scotland Ltd (1 December 1978 to 31 March 1980) the principal activities of NYOS are listed simply:

> to promote musical education and training of persons up to the age of 21 in Scotland;
> to form a Youth Orchestra or other musical ensembles.

To have brought NYOS into being and – before even the first Report and Accounts were completed – into two courses with concerts in 1979 and 1980 was some achievement, not least on the part of William Webb, the first administrator.

In June of 1979 NYOS council had been informed that at the Scottish National Orchestra's new headquarters NYOS would be able to have one room all to itself. The following year Webb, pointing out that he and his assistant were not always in the NYOS office, was asking council to approve the installation of an answerphone, at a cost of £3.55 per week. While the administrative infrastructure of NYOS still depended on resources so meagre, Webb was reporting to council on plans for the 1980 summer course, on the planning of courses over the following two years and on much else. He led a busy life.

December 1978. The founding of NYOS formally announced when Professor Donald Pack, NYOS chairman, receives cheque for £5,000, first instalment of a £20,000 pump-priming grant from Carnegie UK Trust. *Left to right*: Colin MacLean, NYOS vice-chairman; William Webb, NYOS administrator; Professor Pack; Mrs Catherine Sharp, trustee of the Carnegie UK Trust; Geoffrey Lord, secretary and treasurer of the Trust.

Richard Chester, NYOS administrator, then director 1987–

Iain Harrison, NYOS chairman 1994–2000

Alan Simpson, NYOS
chairman 2000–

1980. Tour of Highlands and
Northern Isles. Elizabeth Fyfe, a
founder member of NYOS, oboe
soloist, receives bouquet from
Polly Williams.

1982. Viking Tour. Nicholas Braithwaite, conductor,
in rehearsal with Nigel Kennedy, soloist.

Summer Tour 1986. Sir Alexander
Gibson, conductor (hon. president
NYOS), with Krzysztof Smietana,
soloist.

1992. Mysie Ferguson, violin teacher
employed by NYOS and Highland Region,
initiates workshops and string tuition for
children in Lochaber.
(Courtesy of *Press & Journal*)

August 1979. The first NYOS symphony orchestra.
(Courtesy of the *Daily Record*)

Summer Tour 1995. Evelyn Glennie in Orkney, rehearsing premier of percussion concerto, *African Sunrise–Manhattan Rave* by Dave Heath. A member of NYOS 1981 and 1982, Evelyn Glennie was to be soloist with NYOS in 1987, 1988, 1992 and 1995.

1997. Nicola Benedetti, age nine, leader of NCOS at inaugural public performance in Queen's Hall, Edinburgh. In 2002 Nicola Benedetti was soloist with NCOS for Dvorak's Romance for Violin and Orchestra.

New Year 2002. Garry Walker conducts NYOS symphony orchestra.
A NYOS cellist from 1990 to 1992, he was also a member of
Camerata Scotland.

Colin Currie, in NYOS percussion section from 1990 to 1994, has been
booked as soloist with NYOS for 2005 New Year concerts. In 1994 he
became the first percussion finalist in the BBC Young Musician of the
Year competition.

COMPOSERS

Left to right: John McLeod 1980, 1982, 1987, 1988, 2001;
Edward McGuire 1990, 1992; Thomas Wilson 1993

Rory Boyle 1998   Edward Harper 1993, 2000

John Maxwell Geddes 2001   Gordon McPherson 2002

Other Musical Ensembles

With the support especially of the chairman, also of the finance and general purposes committee plus a great deal of BP back-up, Webb – first with Sandra Davidson, then Eva Flannery as assistant – planned two courses and concerts per year. Distinguished conductors and able tutors were recruited and there were experiments with soloists; some were orchestra members and some were professionals, including the young Nigel Kennedy (for the 1981 New Year concerts and for the 1982 Viking Tour).

NYOS moved around Scotland and out to the islands, then to Scandinavia in 1982, to the Edinburgh Festival in 1983, to Germany and Luxembourg in 1985, to its first BBC London Prom and a second visit to the Edinburgh Festival in the summer of 1988. In the 1988 Summer Concert programmes there appeared for the first time 'Patron: HRH The Prince Edward'. With the help of Lady Aberdeen an approach had been made by Professor Pack to the prince in 1987, an approach the prince was pleased to accept: he attended the 1988 BBC London Prom and afterwards at a reception in the Albert Hall for sponsors, guests and players he established what has become his regular practice on such occasions, of devoting most of his time and attention to the young players.

By 1987 William Webb had moved on to be deputy director of the London College of Music. It had been a decade of rapid consolidation and advance.

From the start NYOS had been committed to undertaking the principal activities, as listed above. It had indeed promoted and advanced the musical education and training of persons up to the age of 21 in Scotland, it had formed a youth orchestra and also some small musical ensembles. Over the next decade remarkable new meaning would be given to 'other musical ensembles'.

Fortunately, Richard Chester was available in 1987 to become the new administrator. Born and educated in Yorkshire, and a graduate of the Royal Academy of Music in London, he had come to Scotland in 1967 to join the Scottish National Orchestra and for 14 years he had been its principal flautist, also one of its directors for six years. As soon as he became administrator of NYOS he was responsible for the auditioning of applicants, in which role he became especially aware of the several handicaps from which many of the young players suffered.

NURTURING TALENT

Though they had reached the recommended Grade VII level they were failing to win a place in the orchestra because it was obvious that they had little or no experience of playing works from the classical repertoire within a demanding orchestral setting. But clearly they showed promise. So Chester argued for the provision of a training course in which these players – up to half of those who had failed to gain places in the large orchestra – could have the benefit of specialist tutoring, leading up to the experience of playing challenging music in a sizeable chamber orchestra.

Eventually Chester added to the symphony orchestra application form 'Please tick if application is only for Easter Course'. This move was intended to encourage diffident students to apply for audition: several who have 'ticked' have in fact proved good enough to go straight into the symphony orchestra. The first repertoire course for string players was held in Oxenfoord Castle School at Easter in 1989. By 1992 there was also an annual Easter course for wind players. Some courses were held in St Leonard's School for Girls, St Andrews, then until Easter 2002 they were all held at the St Andrew's Campus at Bearsden.

Chester then decided to tackle another serious gap in the training and supply of young instrumentalists: there were areas of Scotland where little or no tuition was available. The geographical distribution of applicants for NYOS was noticeably patchy. And it was clear to Chester, as from the start it had been to Webb, that the success of many applicants for places in NYOS depended less on their innate musicality than on the quality of their tuition. Instrumental tuition is not easily provided, certainly not on a wide range of instruments, in remote highland and island regions.

Back in 1947 the director of education for Shetland had written to the NYOGB's Ruth Railton: 'We have plenty of talent here, but no instrumental teachers [. . .] you will always be welcome to help our young musicians.'[1] As soon as NYOS itself was formed, Shetland and Orkney were generously inviting NYOS to use their new hostels and to provide concerts on the islands. The invitations were accepted in 1980, in which year Orkney provided one bassoon player, Allan Buchan, for the orchestra. Over the next two decades Orkney would provide seven players – on bassoon, clarinet, trombone, trumpet and violin. By 1991 NYOS was providing positive financial help; the 1992 annual NYOS report tells that, following a request from Orkney Islands council, NYOS had confirmed financial support of £4,250 towards the provision of string tuition in selected Orkney island schools from December 1991 until June 1992 – and British Airways threw in a couple of free air tickets. But how many tutors can reasonably be supported by an island's council and for how many instruments?

By 1981 Shetland had provided an oboist, Julie Smith, and in the next two decades would provide four players for NYOS – oboe, violin, cello and flute. Meantime, in the early 1980s, from the Isle of Lewis came one percussionist, Elizabeth Fingland.

In the 1980s some parts of mainland Scotland had not been strongly represented by applicants for NYOS. One such was the Lochaber area where the provision of string teaching had been predominantly traditional rather than classical. Chester proposed to NYOS council in 1990 that a full-time violin/viola teacher be funded to work in and from Fort William, serving both primary and secondary schools. The Highland Regional Council agreed to join NYOS in funding the project. On 1 January 1992 Mysie Ann Ferguson took up her post.

The start of the Ferguson regime was marked by careful publicity in the area, by a sizeable band of eager learners, then by concerts at which progress was confirmed by the sometimes laborious, sometimes lively playing of *Twinkle Twinkle Little Star* by small children on minuscule instruments. Mysie Ferguson was succeeded in turn by Cathie Johnson and Nick Hadwen. By the end of the decade Lochaber players whose early tuition had begun with Mysie Ferguson were auditioning at several levels for NYOS ensembles, some playing in the main orchestra. The labours of these Lochaber teachers have contributed to, and complemented, the work of Lochaber Music School which runs a weekly music centre, also workshops and weekends in and around Lochaber. The School caters for players of all ages and ability and fosters interest in both classical and traditional music.

When Richard Chester visits Orkney and Shetland for auditions he also meets staff in the islands' education departments. Following recent requests for back-up with instrumental tuition in the islands NYOS has helped to arrange and finance workshops, some of these directed by Mysie Ferguson, who is now on the staff of Edinburgh Academy.

Major proposals for developments in the work of NYOS were considered at a NYOS council meeting in November of 1991. Mysie

Ferguson's appointment and support for string teaching in Orkney were recorded. Richard Chester reported discussions with Music Advisers in Fife, Highland, Grampian, and Dumfries and Galloway. Already discussions with Fife had resulted in a proposal for an in-service course for music teachers, a course of ten days over the academic year at a cost of £4,000, this to be shared by NYOS, Fife Regional Council and the Arts in Fife. However, the main item on the agenda for that council meeting had the simple heading 'Jazz Course and Chamber Orchestra Course'. Papers and draft budgets were tabled. The chairman and the administrator outlined the cases for the two projects.

There had been a meeting in Edinburgh, called by NYOS, of parties interested in jazz education. Chester spoke of the strong support he had received for the proposal that NYOS might set up a four-day course for about 50 students. Potential for funding was not considered high but it was hoped that pump-priming might be secured and that local authorities would support the proposal. Council approved the jazz project. The National Youth Jazz Orchestra of Scotland (NYJOS) was on its way.

Richard Chester then proposed a four-day course for the most senior students of NYOS, arguing that the potential quality of such an orchestra would be high. The opportunity to perform chamber orchestra works would be valuable and senior NYOS players were keen on the idea. This would be a non-residential course in the Easter holidays, with the students participating in the organisation. No fees would be charged. Council approved the project. The inaugural concerts of the Chamber Orchestra, under the direction of William Conway, took place in April of 1992 in the Stevenson Hall, Glasgow, and the Queen's Hall, Edinburgh; Spring Concerts in 1993 were in Glasgow and Aberdeen. Then the orchestra was engaged in an invitation tour to the 1993 World Youth Orchestra Festival in Japan. In 1994 the orchestra played in Fort William and Kelso, then it joined with LASMO in a concert at which students from music colleges in the UK competed for the LASMO Staffa Music Award – for which NYOS provided auditions and administration. The adjudicators for this, the first, competition were Lady Barbirolli, Lady Aberdeen and Richard Baker.

In 1996 the Chamber Orchestra gave a successful concert at Snape Maltings Concert Hall as part of the Aldeburgh Snape Proms. By 1997 the orchestra had its new name – Camerata Scotland – and was collaborating with Camerata Australia in a major exchange project as part of the New Images Festival. In the summer of 1999 Camerata Scotland travelled to the Netherlands by invitation, for two sell-out concerts at Theatre Aan De Parade, s'Hertogenbosch and at the Concertgebouw, Amsterdam. It continued to partner the LASMO Staffa Award occasions until 2001, when LASMO sponsorship ended. NYOS Council decided that NYOS should undertake sponsorship as well as administration of the Staffa Awards. In April 2002 the first NYOS Staffa Awards concert was held in Queen's Cross Church, Aberdeen, the evening being shared as before with Camerata Scotland. Queen's Cross Church, which has been adapted for concert use as well as worship, offers an excellent venue for such occasions. On this occasion two viola players and a clarinetist competed, the winner of the first NYOS Staffa Award being Wouter Raubenheimer (viola). Born in South Africa, he was a student at the RSAMD, Glasgow. Christoph Mueller conducted Camerata Scotland for the second part of the evening, with Brahms' Serenade No. 1 Opus 11 in D major.

It had been agreed in 1991 that the existing NYOS age limit would apply with the new chamber orchestra, but that limit was soon abandoned, for very good reasons. Camerata Scotland has become a most valuable bridge between the amateur and the professional – the professional worlds of orchestral playing and of music teaching. For players still at music conservatoires and universities it provides invaluable experience in the classical chamber orchestra repertoire. For young music teachers, as for those – no matter their chosen professions – who wish to maintain their instrumental skills, Camerata Scotland offers support as they look around, wherever their careers may take them, to see what amateur orchestras are available. Camerata Scotland has gone from strength to strength: it has given professional strength to its players and it has provided a new sector of strength to the musical life of Scotland.

With the development of Camerata Scotland, education and performance experience was now being provided for senior players, many of them above 21 years of age. NYOS and NYJOS held the lower age limit to 12. Then in the mid-1990s NYOS Council decided to improve its provision for those in the lower age range, from eight to fourteen years old. The result was to become numerically the largest unit in the NYOS company.

The first course for the National Children's Orchestra of Scotland (NCOS) was held in April 1996 with James Durrant and Lewis Morrison in charge. The course ended with an informal performance in Merchiston Castle School, Edinburgh. James Durrant was director of the courses in 1997 and 1998, both of these concluding with a public performance. The number of applicants for NCOS rose rapidly: for the 2002 course 243 students applied, of whom 138 were chosen for NCOS.

The inaugural public performance was in the Queen's Hall, Edinburgh, in 1997. NCOS continued to give spring concerts there until 2000, latterly under the direction of Nigel Murray. In 1998 the scope of NCOS projects was expanded to provide a Preliminary Weekend Training Course where students could become acquainted with the proposed repertoire, with the conductor and tutors and with each other. In 2001 an additional NCOS summer course was introduced in response to demand.

A String Training Course was also established for promising young players who did not quite reach the standard for entry to NCOS: many students who attend this course are invited to play in NCOS in subsequent years. Kenny Mathieson commented on NCOS in the *TES* Scotland:

> What was most impressive was not so much the technical accomplishment of the players, some of whom have not yet even graduated to full-size instruments, as their willingness to express the character of the music, rather than simply doggedly playing the notes.[2]

In April 2001 NCOS combined with Camerata Scotland to present a spring concert in Glasgow's Royal Concert Hall, attended by the Earl and Countess of Wessex. NCOS, with over 130 members, provided the first half of the concert, concluding with 4 young soloists, aged 13 to 17, performing in Bach's Concerto in A minor for 4 Pianos. Camerata Scotland, under Gerard Korsten, provided the second half. There was another joint Camerata–NCOS concert in Glasgow in 2002, this time with Nicola Benedetti as soloist with the NCOS for Dvorak's Romance for Violin and Orchestra. She 'displayed a maturity far beyond her years', said the *Herald* critic.[3] Nicola had been, at the age of nine, leader of the NCOS when it gave its inaugural public performance in 1997, the year she joined the Yehudi Menuhin School in Surrey. She has also appeared as soloist with the London Mozart Players, with the RSNO and with the Warsaw Sinfonia at Birmingham Symphony Hall. In an ITV programme in August 2002 she was named Britain's Most Brilliant Prodigy of the Year.

The first NYOS jazz course was held at Strathallan School for four days in July 1992. It was open – no auditions – to all comers. From the start of NYJOS, generous financial support was given by the Scottish Arts Council and the Musicians' Union. The first course director was Richard Michael, who had pioneered the teaching of jazz to a wide range of pupils in Fife schools. Six professional jazz instrumentalists joined the course to give – sometimes elementary – instruction and take section rehearsals. There was an informal concert on the last day of the course. Likewise in 1993, and in 1994, when a big band (well, comparatively big) was formed, including three guest students from the Faroe Islands. Courses continued under Richard Michael at Strathallan till '97, the '96 course having led up to the first public performance by NYJOS, at the macRobert Arts Centre, Stirling University. By this time 70 young players were involved, and throughout the year jazz courses, workshops, master-classes and tutorials were provided in several regions.

In 1998 Michael shared direction with Nikki Yeoh who for that year was composer-in-residence: part of her composition 'Quiet Freedom' was premiered at the July concert and again performed at courses in October '98 and March '99 (in '99 at Eden Court, Inverness). The complete commission was played by NYJOS at the macRobert Centre in July 1999.

The NYJOS programme for 1998 read:

> The NYJOS faculty of jazz tutors and practitioners have travelled throughout Scotland, bringing the delights of swing, be-bop and beyond to hundreds of music students in a series of jazz workshops organised in collaboration with local authorities and supported by the Bank of Scotland. Their highly successful journey has taken them to the Borders, Ayrshire, Angus and Inverness.

Nurturing Talent

By this stage the week-long NYJOS summer course accommodated both NYJOS proper and also training groups and ensembles for students on the verge of entry to NYJOS. Additional weekend training courses were held when time, funding and performance opportunities permitted. In 2000, NYJOS performed with Jools Holland for BBC *Music Live* in Glasgow's Princes Square shopping centre. In 2001, following a weekend course in January, NYJOS performed to a full and enthusiastic house at the Lemon Tree in Aberdeen. A NYJOS quintet played in the exhibition hall of Glasgow's Royal Concert Hall for the NCOS–Camerata Spring Concert in 2001. NYJOS took part in the Bank of Scotland Edinburgh Jazz and Blues Festivals at the Hub, Edinburgh in July 2001 and July 2002. It also played in Haddington in the spring of 2002.

There have been several directors of NYJOS courses since Richard Michael created the foundations of NYJOS. In '98, '99 and 2000 Eddie Severn directed. By January 2001 there were three directors. In 2001 the course director was Simon Purcell, of the Guildhall School of Music and Drama: he was supported by ten tutors. Eighteen students were listed as NYJOS members; a further 32 attended the course and also performed at the summer concert in the macRobert Centre. Early in 2002, at two induction days, jazz applicants were assessed by professional tutors and allocated, some to comparatively basic training, others to the main NYJOS, this in anticipation of a summer course, following which the main NYJOS went on to play at the Hub for the Edinburgh Jazz Festival.

Meantime, problems of approach and direction were being aired. Richard Chester argued for a reappraisal of auditioning standards for NYJOS courses. The Scottish Arts Council music department, which from the start had been supportive to NYJOS, decided to join in the discussion. NYOS had created a challenge for itself by developing ensembles in what were quite different, possibly conflicting, musical directions.

The 2001 NYJOS Summer Concert programme contained some assertions relevant to the discussion:

> When you go to a classical concert, the focus of attention is likely
> to be the composer, the conductor, soloists and the historical
> context of the music. Tonight, however, the focus will be on the

students and their individual and collective music-making. We will be inviting you to perhaps listen to the music in a different way.

Improvisation has been called the 'sound of surprise', and you will hear contributions from young musicians from 12 to 21. There is a wealth of jazz composers on the staff of this course whose work is included, but it is the magic of improvisation that will bring the concert alive.

The concert will feature some of the new works specially commissioned by NYJOS from five leading Scottish-based composers/musicians. The concert will also feature work from the history of jazz (Ellington, Jelly Roll Morton and Louis Armstrong), contemporary jazz (Arguelles, Bancroft) and some spectacular surprises incorporating all students and tutors in pieces specially written or arranged during the course.

There followed a series of quotations, among them:

The thing that makes jazz so interesting is that each man is his own academy. *Cecil Taylor*

Do not fear mistakes, there are none. *Miles Davis*

Music is your own experience, your thoughts, your wisdom. If you don't live it, it won't come out of your horn. They teach you there's a boundary line to music. But, man, there's no boundary line to art. *Charlie Parker*

When a jazz orchestra was first proposed to NYOS Council in 1991, one argument put forward for the idea was that many able instrumentalists, amateur and professional, are tied to, and confined by, the music on the page before them, and would benefit from tuition in improvisation – a skill that comes naturally only to the lucky few. Improvisation, along with an appreciation of the distinguishing features of jazz, might, it was argued, be required today of professionals if for instance they were engaged for session work, providing backing on popular records. (If, on the other hand, they were to join a jazz group they might find that improvisation would be deemed no more important than the meticulous re-presentation of a standard melody in an arrangement by a noted jazz musician.)

Improvisation had not, of course, originated with jazz nor with any other twentieth-century style of music. The cadenza, the improvisation of the opera singer or of the instrumental soloist, has a long history. Few exponents of improvisation on the organ could be found to match Herrick Bunney, Master of Music at St Giles' Cathedral, Edinburgh, and a member of NYOS' original council.

Discussions throughout 2001 and 2002 focused not only on 'the magic of improvisation' in relation specifically to jazz, but also on the stage of musical development at which improvisation should be taught – or expected.

The SOED Working Paper 6 (1991) had assumed that an activity entitled spontaneous improvisation was to be introduced at a fairly early and elementary stage in education. In the working paper, a proposed outcome was 'Expressing Ideas, Thoughts, Solutions and Feelings':

> Creating and Inventing involves pupils in composition, in the making of arrangements, and in spontaneous improvisation. Through these activities they will find pleasure in sharing and presenting their work, progressing from very simple creations to inventions which show knowledge of structure and a variety of musical skills and style. [. . .]
>
> Pupils may now be beginning to use instrumental sound fairly competently to form inventions which are more structured and varied in tone colour.[4]

The spontaneous inventions or the 'sounds of surprise' in some NYJOS concert performances had for some ears seemed less than pleasing or meritorious.

The meaning or practice of musical improvisation is probably as variable as the definition or practice of jazz, be-bop, swing and beyond, which all create their own variable standards, their own authorities – and elites. Concepts of liberation are associated by many in the jazz world as much with the history, and the historical contexts, of jazz as with its practice. Those who now teach jazz in schools and colleges appear at times to have created a jazz of their own, which may have grown in part from the taxing experience of trying to stimulate in young pupils some initial interest in and pleasure from the instruments made available to music departments. At all levels of music-making, both freedom and discipline may in their different ways offer access to pleasure and to a sense of liberation.

Membership of the symphony orchestra and of the chamber orchestra has sometimes overlapped with that of NYJOS. There has been no overlap of tutors, nor to any degree of audiences. Standards for auditioning and acceptance were not comparable or consistent within the NYOS family. Following extended reappraisal of policies, in 2002 it was decided that auditions for NYJOS courses in 2003 would be more exacting than hitherto, a move which coincided happily with an invitation for NYJOS to travel abroad for the first time – to Holland; this was on the invitation of Tom Odems who had been responsible for the first visits there by NYOS in the mid-1980s.

VI

Application Invited

'She was in the Repertoire Course last year. She's walking into NYOS this year,' says a relaxed Richard Chester after a young violinist has closed the door behind her and set off for home. She must now await audition results which, the application form says, 'will be made known by the end of February'.

The applicant has played two works of her own choice. They were contrasted, according to requirements, in period, tempo and style. The official accompanist, whom she has never seen before, hasn't worried her, even when for a brief spell he drowned her out.

The professional string player sitting at a table alongside Chester has been busily completing an audition form. He puts down his pen and leans back: 'Yes, I liked that. Easy style. Technique OK.'

If only it were always so straightforward.

Over some eight or nine winter weeks Chester, along with another instrumentalist – in strings, woodwind, brass, etc. – sits in ten-minute judgement, morning and afternoon. At the piano on the other side of the young applicant sits the accompanist ready for the next young player and for the next couple of pieces. The accompanist is an accomplished sight-reader and usually knows nearly all that is likely to be offered: Mozart, Bach, Vivaldi, Haydn, Mozart again, Hamilton Harty, Elgar, Weber, Bax, Poulenc, Scott Joplin . . . Scott Joplin – oh! Scott Joplin again. And again! That must be the piece, contrasting in period, tempo and style, favoured by the tutor of this group of players. Little in a day of auditioning will surprise accompanist or judges, except perhaps for 'Why on earth did he choose these two pieces? I can't think of anything more difficult to play for an audition.' Or 'D'you think their teacher encourages all of her pupils to hold their arms like that? Must give them sore shoulders.'

All application forms for auditions must be sent to the NYOS office in Glasgow – before mid-September for the Children's Orchestra and by the end of November for the symphony orchestra. The forms ask how long applicants have been learning their main instrument; and for the seniors, which works they have recently been studying, and are they playing currently with an orchestra or ensemble? Signatures are required, where applicable, from school head teacher, instrumental teachers; and parent or guardian.

The audition process has been extended in several ways since William Webb organised the first series for the first course. On 27 March 1979 he reported to the council that approximately 400 candidates had been auditioned in five cities – Aberdeen, Dundee, Edinburgh, Glasgow and London; the services of seven pianists had been employed; Webb had been accompanied by Peter Mountain (strings), Edgar Williams (wind), Glyn Bragg (percussion) and for the London auditions by Nicholas Kraemer. The council minute continued:

> As an illustration of the overall standard of the orchestra the administrator listed bodies from which candidates had been turned down. Not even all the ex-members of the National Youth Orchestra of Great Britain had been selected.

Since the early 1990s Richard Chester has gone to Orkney and Shetland when anyone there has wished to audition. From November through to February he is in Aberdeen, Inverness, Dundee, Edinburgh, Glasgow, London and Manchester. For most of these, Eva Flannery, the administrator is with him, in charge of audition forms, entrances and exits, phone messages ('Stuck in traffic', 'Cancelled') and coffee and sandwiches. To all these centres come players from near and far, from teachers accomplished and otherwise, from homes richly supportive and informed, or from homes perhaps new to the strange business of instrumental tuition, of orchestras and auditions.

Few halls or rooms available for auditions are especially inviting, least of all in mid-winter. College or church halls, in a strange city, English or Scottish, are usually dull and uninviting. Two floors up in the Central Halls at Edinburgh's Tollcross, or in any city centre, if it is raining or snow is falling outside there is likely to be a constant hiss from traffic on the wet streets below. Car alarms, ambulances, police cars, all create a distracting disharmony. Young players travelling 50 miles, much of it in the dark, from and to their homes, come heavily burdened with bulky trainers or boots, with layers of woollens, fleeces and anoraks, often with a watchful parent in tow. Ten testing minutes of performance in a strange hall or room. Wood panelling and rafters creak unpredictably. Commitment and dedication have been severely tried before the music starts.

An official accompanist is always in attendance at auditions – except for percussion and harp auditions. Chester hopes that applicants will submit themselves to the sometimes exacting experience of the strange accompanist – an added test but a worthwhile one. Some applicants bring their own accompanist, which can sometimes result in a performance that appears awkwardly over-rehearsed.

A young girl painfully lacking in assurance, first time ever at an audition, this one for the Children's Orchestra, finishes her second piece with admirable flourish – light, lively and lovely. She is unmistakeably musical. She looks wide-eyed at the two strangers scribbling at their tables. They ask her to sight-read a few bars of music. Who ever liked a sight-reading test! She hesitates her way fearfully through this ordeal.

Then Chester looks up, smiling kindly: 'Who is your teacher? Been with her long? Do you have any opportunity to play with an orchestra? That lovely Elgar you played, do you know the concerto it comes from? Have you ever been to a concert to hear a large orchestra? Do you listen to recordings of music like that at home?'

What are the conclusions to be reached from the answers to such questions? How to encourage the patently able but conspicuously inexperienced? How to differentiate poor teaching from poor performance?

Garry Walker – member of NYOS in the 1990s, conductor of NYOS ten years later for New Year concerts, in which the main item of the programme was Mahler's Symphony No. 1 – recalls that his mother bought him a recording of this symphony when he was seven. He was then obsessed by the symphony and in 2002 NYOS gave him his first opportunity to conduct it.[1] So should all parents, or schools, aim to detect aptitude at an early age? Might some young applicants prove to be late but able developers?

A boy in his late teens auditions for the symphony orchestra. He plays with forceful competence. He won a place in NYOS last year, in spite of not having a Grade VII. 'Have you passed Grade VII yet?' Chester asks hopefully.

'No, not yet. I've left school. I'm in full-time employment. I'm trying to get enough time off to practise. I really want to go to a music college. I'm working hard at my second instrument and that takes a lot of time.'

He may pass for NYOS again but will he get into a good music college?

He is followed by a girl, same age, sixth year at school, Grade VIII in two instruments. She sails through the audition in relaxed style. She has acceptances already for three colleges, a bursary offered by one of them. Of course she passes for NYOS, probably for Camerata too.

While the staff of the National Youth Jazz Orchestra of Scotland began by operating a comparatively open policy for admission to NYJOS, NYOS has always devoted appreciable resources to its processes of selection for the symphony orchestra. Likewise now for NCOS.

Choice must be made from nearly 250 applicants for over 130 places in NCOS. Up to 400 applicants compete for 120 NYOS places. So which applicants should be invited to the NCOS String Training Course, and which to the NYOS Easter Repertoire Course? To whom say 'Please come again' because distant promise, or determined application, is perceived? Some borderline applicants may be lucky, being accepted partly because there is a shortage of players for a particular section of the orchestra.

Should geographical distribution of applicants be noted and acted upon? Yes, but keeping careful records means still more work for the admin staff. Just why do so many applicants keep coming from, say, Aberdeen and Edinburgh in comparison with Dundee; or Aberdeenshire in comparison with the Lothians? To whom does or should the NYOS director turn in the hope of rectifying the imbalances?

NYOS Applicants 2003

Aberdeenshire	28	E. Renfrew	14	Orkney	3
Aberdeen	33	Edinburgh	46	Perth & Kinross	13
Argyll & Bute	4	Falkirk	4	Renfrewshire	10
Angus	6	Fife	25	S. Ayrshire	18
Borders	5	Glasgow	34	S. Lanarkshire	7
Clackmannanshire	0	Highland	18	Shetland	13
Dundee	9	Inverclyde	9	Stirling	7
Dumfries & Gallo.	6	Mid Lothian	5	W. Dumbarton	3
E. Ayrshire	4	Moray	5	W. Isles	0
E. Dumbarton	10	N. Ayrshire	2	W. Lothian	9
E. Lothian	6	N. Lanark.	4		

Total Applicants: 360

NCOS Applicants 2003

Aberdeenshire	22	E. Renfrew	8	Orkney	9
Aberdeen	23	Edinburgh	49	Perth & Kinross	11
Argyll & Bute	9	Falkirk	0	Renfrewshire	3
Angus	7	Fife	4	S. Ayrshire	8
Borders	1	Glasgow	17	S. Lanarkshire	6
Clackmannanshire	1	Highland	10	Shetland	8
Dundee	1	Inverclyde	3	Stirling	3
Dumfries & Gallo.	0	Mid Lothian	1	W. Dumbarton	2
E. Ayrshire	1	Moray	6	W. Isles	0
E. Dumbarton	13	N. Ayrshire	7	W. Lothian	3
E. Lothian	2	N. Lanark.	2		

Total Applicants: 240

APPLICATION INVITED

For 25 years NYOS has, by means of its programme of auditions, been tuning in to the products of instrumental tuition throughout Scotland. This NYOS activity is unique: no other organisation surveys and serves the Scottish music scene as NYOS does, annually and comprehensively. Comprehensively in both a positive and negative sense: the auditions indicate the highs and lows in the quality of instrumental tuition in Scotland, they also show clearly where and to what extent tuition is in fact available; which localities may have little traditional interest in classical music; which local authorities cater encouragingly for exceptional ability in specialist units or schools; which authorities have chosen to cut out all free instrumental tuition in their primary schools; which authorities provide tuition – but in how many instruments? Only for those whose parents can pay? It may seem that a local authority secondary school has an orchestra of quality, but this may depend on the singular ability and application of one teacher combined with the fact that the tuition of all the orchestra members is funded by parents.

If the very costly monitoring of young players by NYOS is to serve any purpose other than the recruitment into NYOS courses of able and promising instrumentalists, the results of the monitoring must be analysed and then lead to constructive conclusions that are communicated to people of influence. The conclusions may vary from year to year, depending in large measure on changing attitudes within changing locations of power (local and national). These have not been static in the past 25 years.

Central to the thinking of the group who brought NYOS into existence in the 1970s, and central to the arguments they deployed in winning support for a Scottish youth orchestra, was (as outlined in Chapter One) the fact that in two previous decades there had been an upsurge of instrumental teaching in many Scottish schools, primary and secondary. The upsurge came about partly because piano playing and school singing were going out of fashion, partly because of an increased availability of instruments at affordable prices, but mainly because there was a period of political will at the top – from people like Jennie Lee and Edward Heath. The upsurge had, as ever, been uneven in origin and impact, not least because local authorities had markedly differing attitudes to the arts.

Regional government came and went, so educational power bases moved from the local to the regional, then in the 1990s back to the local. In 1999 came the Scottish Parliament and an executive in which personnel and policies have taken time to settle.

Over the past 25 years political policies and ministers' preferences have varied greatly. In the course of the 1980s there was a tendency to economise in instrumental tuition, more in England than in Scotland. In 1991 the Scottish Office Education Department issued Expressive Arts 5–14, signed by Michael Forsyth.[2] In this document music shared expressive space with art and design, drama, and physical education. The sections on music gave prominence to expression, to critical appreciation and appraisal, also to singing, the voice as ever being an instrument involving no purchase costs for authority or pupil. As for other instruments, the paper assumed a general availability of various categories of percussion, an understandable provision as so much percussion withstands vigorous and inexpert treatment.

Rhythm may well be the basis of music, but to some with sensitive hearing it may now seem that percussion, at one stage (as John Dalby said) the Cinderella of orchestral music, has become the Ugly Sister of the family of sound – rumbling, beating, or crashing, not only in the wider field of popular music-making but also through so much that is heard on radio and television and in all manner of entertainment. 'Activities such as "How many different sounds can you make with a drum?" help to widen the children's imagination,' said the SOED paper unfeelingly.[3]

The paper assumed availability in school and home of keyboards, most of which have much more percussive potential than the pianos of yesteryear. Among the paper's 'Aims Specific to Music' was that of encouraging all pupils to realise their musical potential. It assumed class or school productions in which

> the emphasis shifts from the developmental learning process to a highly disciplined, organised and polished activity which is often planned from the outset as something which will be publicly performed.[4]

The highly disciplined activity, by pupils, of playing a range of musical instruments was apparently to be a resource upon which teachers would rely, whatever the source.

APPLICATION INVITED

Teachers have to manage the human resources available, including their own deployment. They need to be aware of the resources beyond the school and be able to make use of them to enrich the programme.[5]

At this stage (Level E2) the number and range of instruments available may increase. Any individual children who are learning to play an instrument should be encouraged to participate in class, as this can enhance class ensemble playing.[6]

The matter of where and how individual children were learning to play an instrument was not explored in the SOED paper.

At this time new systems of instrumental instruction were being introduced in England and Wales, systems which in the main were resulting in a reduction of instruction and in costs being passed on to parents. So it was understandable and timely that in 1993 heads of instrumental teaching in Scotland issued a position paper *Instrumental Instruction in Schools* .[7] This paper referred to what had been a sustained growth over some decades in instrumental provision in Scottish schools, and consequently a growth in school, area and national ensembles. Instrumental services, for some years in some areas, had mainly been free at the point of delivery. Resources, however, had tended to be allocated mostly to schools where it was felt they would be used effectively so, the position paper said, an openly elitist system operated.

The position paper outlined the qualities and characteristics said to be evident in those who had applied themselves to the learning of an instrument and it pointed to the increase in the number of pupils presented for music courses in schools, also in the number studying music in colleges and universities and in the standards of performance in national ensembles. The position paper concluded:

> The quality and range of provision in this country owes much to the fact that it has been organised by local authorities, targeted effectively, normally offered free of charge and supported by a system of instrumental ensembles in which players can develop their full potential.[8]

The targeting may have been effective but it was by definition selective or elitist. If NYOS, therefore, was to be creaming players from that process it, too, would find itself labelled elitist. So in 1994 NYOS invited the media to look at the situation. In a brief overview it said:

> The good provision of music instrumental teaching in Scotland has been built up over recent decades in state schools in Scotland. The present provision is perhaps the healthiest it has been and is held in high regard by countries throughout the world.
>
> With recent changes in the provision of instrumental teaching in England and Wales, Scotland is the only country where such provision is formally and constructively arranged through all the education departments of local authorities.
>
> We are in an enviable position whereby the instrumental teachers in Scotland are not only well managed but also are of the highest possible standard. Teachers are undertaking excellent work, measured by the high standard achieved not only by local authority district and regional orchestra but also by the National Youth Orchestra of Scotland.
>
> A reduction of the provision of music instrumental teaching in Scotland either through a reduction in finance or by local government changes must be avoided at all costs. NYOS supports the excellent work being undertaken by instrumental teachers throughout Scotland and calls on all local government education departments and local councillors to support, continue and develop the excellent provision of instrumental instruction in schools in Scotland.

The *TES* Scotland commented:

> Many of the instruments they teach are horribly expensive to provide, and yet [. . .] no one wants a situation where only parents able to buy tuition and an instrument can have their children taught. [. . .]
>
> There is a danger that the break-up of the regions and the devolution of financial control to headteachers may imperil the startling progress made in the past 20 years, not because anyone

wants that to happen but because existing structures disappear
and there is not the will to replace them.

TES Scotland faced facts: 'In the upheaval which new councils will
bring, the provision of instrumental tuition is not going to strike the
loudest of chords.'[9]

Now the regions have gone. The Scottish Parliament has come. More
upheaval. Chords of all sorts. Volume has varied. Policy documents
have been issued. Still, local councils have widely varying priorities and
always limited resources. Politicians, local and national, have argued.
Comparatively few (Donald Dewar was an exception) have shown
personal enthusiasm for the arts in general or music in particular, or
classical music in the more particular.

Meantime NYOS has strained to find the necessary resources to
maintain its work, not least to welcome to its auditions, for places in
NYOS and now NCOS, around 600 young players aged 8 to 21. From
the 600, it aims to provide places in these orchestras for around 250
players and, in addition, it offers, in training courses, orchestral
experience and specialist tutoring for more than 100 of the others. The
specialist tutoring involves each year over 100 of the best instrumental
teachers available in Scotland, many of them members of Scotland's
professional orchestras.

In recent years NYOS has sought out, and then channelled, resources
not only for improving the quality and quantity of instrumental tuition,
especially in areas of deprivation, or (as the New Labour term has it) of
cultural exclusion, it has also pioneered projects in a number of nursery
and primary schools in the hope of detecting and encouraging young
children who already at three or four years of age are showing signs of
musical promise. The John Lewis Partnership has generously funded
NYOS in much of the administering of such projects. In order to
improve the quality of provision in certain areas NYOS has – drawing
on its audition findings – arranged for personnel to give master-classes
to both students and teachers.

The existence of NYOS orchestras offers in itself an incentive for
young players and for their instrumental teachers. The training courses,
the tutoring and the orchestral experience in these orchestras have now
for some years fed back into Scotland's regional and school orchestras

an increasingly high standard of instrumental and orchestral playing. Whereas in 1979 Scotland's new youth orchestra gained necessary strength by drawing on the talent available among specialist college students, especially from the Royal Scottish Academy of Music and Drama, now NYOS is feeding into these colleges a greatly improved quality of entrant, and at the same time providing in its courses, and especially in Camerata Scotland, a continuing experience, for these students, of participation in the classical repertoire, an experience invaluable for them, not least if they are progressing to employment with the major symphony or chamber orchestras.

NYOS provides strongly educational services. It also contributes to the cultural life of Scotland. It may be said to perform some of the work of an educational inspectorate. It points, as tactfully as possible, to some of the deficiencies in educational provision. It feeds, at several levels, into several sectors of musical activity in Scottish society. Through its steadily expanding programme of initiatives, of auditions, training courses and – not least – its performances, it provides a remarkably pleasurable service. After the first NYOS course in 1979 William Webb reported to the Council:

> Although the schedule of rehearsals had been very strenuous, there had been no complaints from the members on this count. Indeed, even though they were asked to play for some seven hours a day, they were still willing to play chamber music in their spare time. Their appetite for music was apparently insatiable.

In addition to meeting the requirements of the education and the arts establishments, NYOS has been eager to satisfy as many musical appetites as possible. Always there is the hope that concert audiences – and of course the critics – are happy with what they hear. It is assumed that applicants who are accepted for training and performance are glad to be accepted: the tutorial and house staffs work hard to ensure that the musical appetites of the students continue to be insatiable.

In much, though not all, of NYOS work there is a commitment to the pursuit of excellence. Alas, of approximately 700 applicants for places in NYOS ensembles some are disappointed. There's always next year. And if NYOS can raise the money it may one day be able to cater appropriately and pleasurably for all comers.

And Then . . .

NYOS SOLOIST
Elizabeth Fyfe, from Stirling, a founder member of NYOS, was a soloist for the 1980 Tour of the Highlands and Northern Isles, playing Mozart's Oboe Concerto in C major K314. She went to Fitzwilliam College, Cambridge, then made a career in music, becoming principal cor anglais in the orchestra of the Royal Opera House, Covent Garden. Now married, with a family of four, she teaches at Wells Cathedral School of Music.

AN AMAZING NUMBER
From an e-mail to Eva Flannery, NYOS Administrator, 17 September 2002.

> Dear Eva
> I thought I had better get in touch and let you know my new address . . . This is my married name, Kathleen Beggin, but I am still professionally known as Kathleen Stevenson.
> Last year I became a member of the Royal Philharmonic Orchestra as Principal Piccolo and have to sit in front of Douglas Mitchell. It is just like old times! It's amazing the number of ex-NYOS members I run into. You're definitely doing something right.
> I hope you and Richard are well.
> Kathleen Stevenson

Kathleen Stevenson, from Paisley, and Douglas Mitchell (clarinet), from Milngavie, were in NYOS from 1984 till 1988.

THE BURKE FAMILY
For 13 years there was always a member of the Burke family in the Viola section of the NYOS symphony orchestra. In 1997 all five were playing in NYOS orchestras, two in the symphony orchestra and three in Camerata Scotland. All five are graduates of Edinburgh University.

Eileen is now a primary classroom teacher in Edinburgh. Aided by a general Teaching Council scholarship, she is studying the promotion of learning through music for young children.

Rosemary teaches violin and viola and has trained as a Suzuki Violin Teacher.

Aidan has worked in Bosnia for several years. He has been co-ordinator there of an international ensemble, and has led a project of creative music workshops in the school for the blind and partially sighted in Sarajevo.

Andrew has been working on a doctorate in environmental science, specialising in archaeological resource management.

David works for Falkirk Council as a secondary school music teacher.

THREE

Performance

VII

The Critic's Angle
CONRAD WILSON

In a vitriolic essay on the vices of music critics, Benjamin Britten once complained that composers and performers were never satisfactorily informed in print about the standards by which they were being judged. Yet the solution, he said, was perfectly simple. All a critic needed to do was to add an explanatory sentence to each review, such as: 'For a first opera – a jolly good shot; for an amateur performance – very creditable'.

It was no great demand, but to have obeyed it would have been to run the risk of seeming detestably patronising. Amateurs, in my experience, do not want to be reminded that they are amateurs, any more than novice composers want to be told they are novices. A good amateur performance, in any case, can be more arresting and more committed than a routine professional one. First operas, like first novels, can be better than second ones. And youth orchestras, I would add, can be judged by standards – nowadays very high standards – which require to be mentioned only if a performance falls perplexingly below them.

Yet, as every critic learns, there are youth orchestras and youth orchestras: new ones and old-established ones; national ones and civic ones; college-of-music ones and high-school ones; moneyed ones and impoverished ones; serious ones and opportunistic ones; disciplined ones and raunchy ones; audacious ones and play-safe ones; well-run ones and disorganised ones; ones that are on the way up and ones that are on the way down; good ones with bad conductors; bad ones with good conductors. All are competing for cash, fame, players, audiences, foreign tours and a spot of space in a newspaper.

Those from countries which care about music and are prepared to pay for it are more likely – though not inevitably – to be superior to those whose every public appearance is a struggle. Sometimes (naming no names) the country of origin will be a large one, with a long orchestral tradition; sometimes it will be a small one, with a sense of pride; and sometimes, no matter what the size, it will be a country which unfortunately regards classical music as irrelevant and prefers to spend its money in a different way. It all depends.

The growth and importance of one particular youth orchestra, the National Youth Orchestra of Scotland, is what, from a critic's viewpoint, concerns me here. Its current members were not even born when the orchestra was founded a quarter of a century ago. Its conductors have largely changed, as have the many dedicated people, most of them senior members of professional orchestras or experienced teachers from the Royal Scottish Academy of Music and Drama, who act as coaches.

It is also a more complex organisation than it was, with various splinter groups – a biggish and valuable chamber orchestra called Camerata Scotland, a brass ensemble, a very racy jazz outfit, a children's orchestra – which also require organising. There are major tours to plan, with Holland and Scandinavia (thanks to their interest in youth orchestras) high on the list, and regular domestic engagements to be worked out – though 'domestic', for these young Scottish-based players, means not only Glasgow, Edinburgh, Aberdeen and Dundee, but also remote Scottish islands and small isolated towns where the only suitable auditorium may be a school hall or gymnasium.

Running the orchestra from its Glasgow office is a full-time operation and an increasingly active one, even if only a handful of concerts are given each year. For these, however, an alert, expert director is needed, attuned to every aspect of recruiting, training, rehearsing, touring and forward planning a youth orchestra of more than a hundred players, with the support of a necessarily expanding staff.

Yet NYOS is not some solitary exotic bloom in infertile soil. It has a context in that there are two long-running festivals of youth orchestras in Scotland, one of them in Aberdeen, the other split between Edinburgh and Glasgow. And that context has a further context, in that many of the players will become professional musicians, some of them as members of full-time orchestras. There is also St Mary's Music School, Douglas Academy, the City of Edinburgh Music School, the Aberdeen City Music School and the National Centre of Excellence in Scottish Music whose close relationship with NYOS is another binding factor.

So the ground keeps shifting, usually beneficially, sometimes less so. Since 1990, Glasgow – and thus also NYOS – has had a big, greatly welcomed new concert hall in the city centre. The smaller City Hall, an acoustically fine but dilapidated setting for Camerata Scotland, is being refurbished, a process already completed in the case of Edinburgh's Usher Hall. On the other hand, in 2002, the players lost the well-equipped college facilities on Glasgow's outskirts that had served for some years as their home and workplace during the intensive weeks of preparation for performances.

Finding the right premises, with plenty of rooms for sectional rehearsals, a space big enough for the full orchestra, comfortable accommodation, an acceptable self-service restaurant and suitable recreation areas, had to begin all over again and, at the time of writing, has yet to be resolved. Yet nothing is more crucial if a hundred young players are to be enticed into giving up school or college holidays for the sake of learning how to perform orchestral music.

Losing the right premises is thus one of the worst hazards faced by the orchestra's director. Tantalisingly, the best facilities of all are those in Orkney, but they are hardly the most accessible. Resourcefulness, however, is an essential element of the arts in Scotland. The first concert NYOS ever gave, we should remember, was in a tent, not in Glasgow or Edinburgh but in Falkirk.

Which is where this critic's contribution to a celebratory book should start some specific celebrating of its own. But first a few possibly tactless questions. What are youth orchestras actually for? Who really wants to hear them? And are they genuinely worth the money and energy spent on them?

Each question could invite a cynical answer. For example: youth orchestras form just another unnecessary part of the music industry. Or for example: youth orchestras perform mostly to please parents, relatives, and friends of the players who, on the orchestra's home ground, form a high proportion of the audience. Or more positively: youth orchestras are 'educational', which means that they are likely to please Tony Blair and prompt him to open his ears, whereas mention of the Royal Scottish National Orchestra's or the Scottish Chamber Orchestra's financial insecurity makes his eyes glaze over.

NYOS, since its foundation in 1979, has survived several British prime ministers and their attitudes. It was not in fact Scotland's first youth orchestra. There were, and still are, others, with the Edinburgh Youth Orchestra as a good example of what was possible within the confines of a single city if someone of James Loughran's calibre was willing to appear as conductor.

The fear, when NYOS was first mooted, was that good players might be lured away from already existent but less-ambitious orchestras – a suspicion similarly aroused by Ruth Railton's long-established London-based National Youth Orchestra of Great Britain. But it was a risk which, in spite of doubts and complaints, needed to be taken, if only, as some realistic observers argued, on the principle that there is no cream without milk.

Perhaps the main point in favour of a Scottish national youth orchestra was that it was simply time to form one. Scotland (or, to be more accurate, a handful of visionary people inside Scotland) had already launched, on hitherto stony ground, a miraculous company called Scottish Opera, a triumphantly successful Edinburgh Festival Chorus, and an increasing (though still, by international standards, quite small) number of orchestras and chamber ensembles of different sizes. The creation of a national youth orchestra, to match those of other countries, was conspicuously overdue.

I myself had the good luck – and the challenge that went with it – to review NYOS' debut concert in the summer of 1979. It was my good luck because I sensed at once that I was witnessing the birth of something special. It was a challenge because I did not want merely to enthuse about what I heard in Falkirk's Callender Park that day (the critic who enthuses, as Bernard Shaw might have said, is lost).

The Critic's Angle

The shortcomings of what was an impressive but by no means flawless event had to be addressed along with the splendours. The obstacles to enjoyment – including the lifeless acoustics of the so-called Big Top, where the concert took place, and the sound of rain drumming on the roof – could not be ignored. Even if they were only passing irritations, they affected the playing and made aspects of it hard to assess. The quality of the string tone had to be taken on trust, because strings invariably fare worse than wind instruments under such conditions. Yet to have described the results as no more than 'very creditable' would have been unjust. By and large they were considerably better than that.

The chosen programme, it's true, took no wild risks. The overture, appropriate to the occasion, was Hamish MacCunn's picturesque *Land of the Mountain and Flood*. The concerto was Mozart's for clarinet, with an established soloist in the person of Janet Hilton, the poetic principal clarinet of the recently formed Scottish Chamber Orchestra. Instead of a symphony there was a pairing of Tchaikovsky's *Romeo and Juliet* and Respighi's *Pines of Rome* – strong, keenly coloured music which, once set in motion, was unlikely to fall apart. The conductor was Nicholas Braithwaite, not one of the big British names, but at any rate the son of an old friend (Warwick Braithwaite, who during the Second World War had been in charge of the Scottish National Orchestra, or Scottish Orchestra as it then was). His primary, most inspirational virtue was that he was as much at ease with a new-minted youth orchestra as with the young Glyndebourne Touring Company, with which he was also working at the time.

Such an ability, as the original organisers of NYOS were quick to perceive, is more vital than star status. It goes (or should do) with understanding, patience, humour, an awareness of how best to use rehearsal time, a way with words, and a command of gesture that derives from knowing how a youth orchestra differs from a symphony orchestra and how subtly the players need to be handled if the best is to be got out of them. As one senior coach succinctly said to me, 'I don't like conductors who talk down to them.'

Planting fear in a youth orchestra is not an option, even if some conductors of an older school – Leopold Stokowski and Paul Tortelier, to mention two I have observed at work with young players – used to believe that an intense performance was dependent on it.

Tortelier, distinguished cellist though he was, clearly had merciless views on how to conduct such orchestras and, on the occasion I heard him, he was spreading terror among members of an orchestra at Vevey, on Lake Geneva. The victim at whom he screamed the most, if I remember rightly, was the first trumpet, who could do nothing to satisfy the veteran musician. Appalled by what I saw and heard, I resolved not to wait for the concert itself, nor to discover whether the trumpeter survived to take part in it.

Stokowski, by then in his extreme old age, was quieter but in some ways even more alarming. Far from treating the National Youth Orchestra of Great Britain as the crème de la crème of young British players, he exhibited lofty disdain at a rehearsal I attended in London in the 1960s. At that point in his career, admittedly, he had become so impatient with any orchestra at all that, if someone drew out a handkerchief or whispered to another player at rehearsal, he or she was likely to be sent off the platform. Like Tortelier, Stokowski focused his distaste on one chosen player, this time a member of the woodwind who, in a Tchaikovsky symphony, was not producing the desired tone quality. The player, I learnt later, was dismissed during the final rehearsal, which was something a conductor of Stokowski's status could do as a matter of routine, making no allowances for the youthfulness of youth orchestras.

So how does NYOS, or at least its director, react to unsuitable or 'difficult' conductors? Avoid them is the short answer – though Richard Chester, the orchestra's current, thoroughly experienced intendant, who had been principal flute of the Scottish National Orchestra before taking up his appointment in 1987, admits that there are a few conductors and soloists who, for one reason or another, have not been invited back. That veto, however, was never applied to Braithwaite, who used to appear almost annually with the orchestra, until the value of ringing the changes began to be discerned.

But there have been others, too, who have established a special affinity with NYOS, one of whom, James Loughran, conveniently resides in Glasgow. Yet it is not just for convenience that he is on Chester's list of

HRH The Earl of Wessex, NYOS patron since 1987, meeting orchestra members at the Summer Concert, 1999.

Glasgow 1999. Competitors for Lasmo Staffa Music Award (standing *left to right*), Timothy Mirfin, Ian Wilson, Ilid Jones and Marko Martin with adjudicating panel (seated *left to right*), Dr Chris Wright, managing director of Lasmo, Richard Baker, Lady Barbirolli, James Loughran.

Sydney 1997. Camerata Scotland toured Australia and UK in
collaboration with Camerata Australia as part of the New Images
Festival to celebrate the British Council's 50th anniversary in Australia.

July 1998. Richard Michael, first director of NYJOS,
in macRobert Arts Centre, Stirling.

NYJOS students in macRobert Arts Centre, July 2001.

1980. In NYOS Tour of the Highlands and Northern Isles, the orchestra gave a concert at the Sullum Voe Terminal, the farthest point north at which a full symphony orchestra has played in the UK. Photo shows orchestra members, tutors, house staff and Council members.

The Burke Family. For 13 years there was always a member of the Burke family in the NYOS viola section. *Left to right*: Rosemary, Eileen, David, Andrew, Aidan.

2001. Wellfield Nursery School, Springburn, Glasgow. With support from John Lewis Partnership NYOS has arranged for the provision of string tuition for three to five year olds at Wellfield, also at St Mary's Primary School, Maryhill, Glasgow, and in Castle Douglas for the Galloway Suzuki Group.

1997. Queen's Hall, Edinburgh. Inaugural public concert of
The National Children's Orchestra of Scotland.

1998. Young players from Ayrshire
in NCOS preliminary Course at St
Andrew Campus, Bearsden.

2002. NCOS, Royal Concert
Hall, Glasgow.

New Year 2003. Royal Concert Hall, Glasgow.
Sian Edwards conducts the NYOS symphony orchestra.

New Year 2003. NYOS, Royal Concert Hall, Glasgow.

acceptable conductors. The fact that he can be away from Scotland for long periods makes him quite hard to pin down. But what makes him worth cultivating is that, like Braithwaite, he can get the best out of young players. Moreover, having been principal conductor of such orchestras as the Halle, the Bamberg Symphony, and the BBC Scottish Symphony, Loughran has wide experience, plenty of interpretative know-how, a penchant for imaginative programmes and a degree of glamour. Now in his seventies, he has grown mellow rather than tyrannical in his old age. But his standards remain high and NYOS rises to them.

Loughran's early success with the Edinburgh Youth Orchestra guaranteed that he would be invited to conduct NYOS also. Working with youth orchestras, he said to me recently, is an experience he greatly enjoys, so long as it is not some unruly outfit from the American Mid-West. Yet it was 1988 before he and NYOS got together, though when they finally did so it was in a series of major performances, including Shostakovich's Fifth Symphony at the London Proms and – at the Edinburgh Festival – Thea Musgrave's theatrical Concerto for Orchestra along with Luciano Berio's witty gloss on Boccherini's *La Ritirata Notturna di Madrid*. Though Musgrave and Berio were new composers for NYOS, Shostakovich was not. As early as 1980, the orchestra had played Shostakovich, coupling his Second Cello Concerto with a Scottish work, John McLeod's *The Shostakovich Connection* (partly inspired by the Fifth Symphony), in a single programme conducted by Edward Downes.

To have described any of these concerts, in deference to Britten, as 'a jolly good shot' would have been a tepid response to something so enthrallingly more than that. The same could be said for the three sensuous tableaux of Ravel's second *Daphnis and Chloe* Suite, transported all the way to Shetland and Orkney in the summer of 1980, or for Stravinsky's *Rite of Spring* – that great cement-mixer of a work, as Simon Rattle once called it – compressed by Nicholas Braithwaite into the cramped space of Dumfries's Academy Hall in 1981.

Making the impossible possible was clearly one of NYOS's aspirations right from the start, when William Webb, from the staff of the SNO, had the same aspirations for the players as Chester would display later. Dumfries had never previously experienced a live *Rite*, nor any other work of its kind in such shattering close-up, and perhaps would never do so again.

To have written that NYOS' performance of *The Rite* (there were in fact three in 1981) was 'very creditable' would have been a thoroughly inadequate response to something that demanded real reaction. To have said that it was better, or worse, than the Scottish National Orchestra's most recent performance of the work would have been assertive but offensive to one orchestra or the other. Simply to say what it was like – how accurate, how pungent, how focused, how explosive, how exciting, how rhythmic, how confident, how truly Stravinskian, how well or badly conducted – was all that really mattered.

Invited to chronicle NYOS's first Shetland adventure exclusively for *The Scotsman*, I felt obliged to accept instantly, lest a rival paper seize the initiative. The offer, in any case, was irresistible, because the trip was something musically so unprecedented. Rather than fly separately to Sumburgh airport, I agreed instead to join the hundred-or-more players and their carers on board the *St Clair* at Aberdeen and journey slowly to Lerwick by sea. It was the right decision. Though this was my 11th big trip with a Scottish orchestra or opera company, and though I was to do 20 more before enough began to seem enough, it was likely, as I surmised, to be a jaunt destined to go down in the annals.

As for the opening concert, the swirl of Wagner's *Flying Dutchman* Overture seemed the most piquant way to set the programme in motion amid the desolate seascapes of Sullom Voe. The Hillside Centre, being the property of an oil company, could hardly be hailed as a custom-built concert hall. But the concert so audaciously presented there made history. It was the most northerly of its kind ever given in Britain.

En route to Lerwick, my cabin on the *St Clair* had been quiet and comfortable, though a fair amount of engagingly impromptu music took place on board. Dinner, as the ship sailed placidly into a Nordic sunset, was idyllic. On deck the conductor, Nicholas Kraemer, conferred amiably with groups of players. Did I say Nicholas Kraemer? But how was a leading British baroque specialist going to deal not only with *Daphnis and Chloe* but also Elgar's *Enigma Variations*, works that lay far outside his now established repertoire? Perhaps in 1980 it seemed less strange than it would today. The answer, in any case, was that it did not seem strange at all, though doubtless the distance from London gave him a sense of freedom.

The performance which really stuck in the memory, however, was that of Mozart's Oboe Concerto, with Elizabeth Fyfe, a member of the orchestra's woodwind section, as an exquisite soloist. This gifted player, I felt disheartened to learn, was going to Cambridge to study something other than music. But in tribute to her beauty of tone, the orchestra played Mozart with a finesse and precision which had eluded them in the Clarinet Concerto the previous year. No doubt the presence of Kraemer, here much closer to his home ground, was helpful also.

Next morning at dawn I was driven to Sumburgh for a flight to Aberdeen, while the orchestra prepared for a concert in Kirkwall, where the programme was to be rejigged to incorporate Peter Maxwell Davies' *Five Klee Pictures*. Since the Manchester-born composer was by then already resident in Orkney, this was one more example of what was becoming predictably astute programme planning on the part of William Webb, the orchestra's first director.

What was less predictable was the weather. Elsewhere in this book, Colin MacLean explains how fog can be a threat to concerts in the Northern Isles, by which, however, the orchestra remains undeterred. My flight southwards, scheduled to make a stopover at Kirkwall, found Orkney fogbound. A Lerwick bookseller, sitting beside me on the aircraft, worriedly informed me that he was due to take a boat from Orkney to the Faroes for his annual holiday. The boat sailed fortnightly and, by the time the aircraft, after circling Kirkwall, finally landed in Aberdeen, he must have had no hope of catching it. The orchestra, booked to fly from Sumburgh to Orkney next day, encountered the same problem. A makeshift boat was hurriedly chartered and the bedraggled players reached Orkney at dawn.

Yet in 1982 the orchestra was itself in the Faroes – and in Orkney, Norway, Sweden, and Denmark as well, with a nautical programme featuring Elgar's *Sea Pictures*, Debussy's *La Mer*, and a new Scottish work, John McLeod's *The Gokstad Ship*. In 1983, Webern's tightly compressed *Six Pieces*, Op. 6, must have seemed even more than usually minimalistic alongside the grandeur of Carl Nielsen's *Inextinguishable* symphony in Stornoway, Inverness, Pitlochry, Aberdeen and Edinburgh, with Christopher Adey, a rightly renowned orchestral trainer and Sir

Alexander Gibson as conductors. This was Gibson's first appearance with the orchestra, but there would be another in 1986 when Iain Hamilton's impressionistic dawn picture, *Aurora*, sustained a radiant trajectory from Torshavn in the Faroes to Stavanger in Norway (in each of which it was performed) and Carl Nielsen's *An Imaginary Journey to the Faroes* served as an imaginative encore.

Reviewing NYOS' concerts in Edinburgh or Glasgow was by then, for me, a regular critical assignment, no less exciting than following the orchestra through Nordic waters. The programmes remained inventive, the standards uncompromisingly high. Each performance spoke eloquently not only for the quality of the players themselves, but also for the quality of the coaching. Each concert – or, let us say, most concerts – could thus be recognised as the vivid outcome of a process which had begun months earlier with auditions and gone on to rehearsals as all these young musicians were gradually shaped into a single instrument upon which a conductor, arriving fairly late in the proceedings, could play.

The old, objective tradition whereby critics avoid meeting the people they criticise can sometimes seem a sound one. But it would be hard to implement in a country as small as Scotland, where last night's performer could be someone you encounter in your local newsagent next morning.

So when Richard Chester recently urged me to sample more than just the public outcome of NYOS's orchestral courses, I did not hesitate to say yes and to see for myself what goes on at auditions, coaching sessions, and sectional rehearsals. Chester himself, as director, meticulously attends all auditions, partly because he is an experienced player, but also because it is clearly so very much his orchestra.

Attending a day of violin auditions in Edinburgh, I noted how some applicants brought along show-pieces which revealed nothing but the fact that the player could play them. Other qualities, however, were being looked for, and when they were present it was easy to spot them. Wrong notes did not denote failure. What mattered were recognisable signs of musicality, perception, instinct and the player's own response to, or recognition of, anything that went wrong.

With a distinguished Edinburgh string player sitting by his side,

Chester would briefly discuss what each applicant had to offer before the next candidate was ushered in. The standard struck me, for the most part, as encouragingly high, but it was those who sailed through Sarasate who seemed, to my ears, out of their depth. What good is an armoury of glissandi and double stoppings if the music to be worked on is a Beethoven symphony?

Youth orchestras achieve their successes, it has been claimed, mainly through sheer weight of numbers. With a huge horn section and a big enough array of strings, Strauss's *Don Juan* may manage to bowl listeners over. But there is more to Strauss's symphonic poem than that, and NYOS, in any case, is just as likely to perform Strauss's Oboe Concerto or *Four Last Songs*, where fastidious delicacy is needed, as one of his brazen tours de force.

For evidence of what really goes into the orchestra's training sessions, I accepted Richard Chester's invitation to eavesdrop on some of these in Glasgow, where Mahler's First Symphony, Bruch's First Violin Concerto and Dvorak's *Carnival* Overture were being gradually pieced together.

Mahler, like Berlioz and Verdi, is a composer often described as noisy, when the reality, much of the time, is actually the opposite. Some of the most inspired moments in Berlioz' Requiem and Verdi's Requiem – and how good it would be, incidentally, to hear NYOS participate sometime in a great choral masterpiece – are the quietest ones. With Mahler's First Symphony it is the same. The slow introduction, with its cuckoo-calls and sense of misty awakening, is nature music of the choicest sort.

After hearing a line-up of flutes practise the art of Mahler articulation, I switched to a neighbouring room where the horns were learning to bring poetry to a short but crucial passage in Max Bruch, with gaps left in the music where other instruments would later join in. It was a good way to be reminded how much these young players have to prepare from scratch in a short space of time. In yet another room, a cluster of string players were coping not only with the notes but with distinctive elements of Mahler style in one of those searing passages which erupt in the finale. Some members of the orchestra, before starting the course, may have known nothing much about Mahler at all. By the end, they would have got to know him very well. For those who hope to become professional orchestral players, NYOS is a perfect training ground. As

James Durrant, one of the most respected coaches, recently put it to me, 'they get a lot of coaching for their money'.

The conductor, who was in the building but not yet at work with the full orchestra, was the Scottish-born Garry Walker, who looked not much older than some of the players and who had recently triumphed in the Leeds International Competition. When, not many days later, the programme reached the Usher Hall, Edinburgh, the whole performance had coalesced. Walker, beating boldly and clearly, left nothing to chance. The Mahler, I thought, needed to be played with more sweep and freedom, especially in the finale, where the string tone lacked its full emotional vibrancy.

A good shot? Again it was more than that. Holding the players on a tight rein proved its worth when the work reached its climax, and Mahler's long-term symphonic argument fell finally into place. Sir Adrian Boult's famous dictum for conductors – that even the biggest symphony should be conducted as if it were spread out across two huge pages of musical score – seemed to have been observed. Walker himself had probably learned a lot about Mahler's First Symphony through conducting this performance of it. The learning process had thus flowed both ways, which seemed an excellent reason for teaming an able, gifted, but still inexperienced young conductor with players who were eager for experience and not yet set in their ways.

But not all of NYOS' conductors are of Walker's youthfulness. Others, like Loughran and Gibson (before his untimely death), bring years of experience, and their own methods of rehearsal, to their role. Some conductors run straight through a symphony before getting down to its nuts and bolts. Others, perhaps more disconcertingly, begin with the nuts and bolts and gradually assemble the performance.

In the winter of 1996, when I was invited by Richard Chester to present a course for would-be music critics side by side with the instrumental coaching sessions in Glasgow, I was permitted to take my class to the first full orchestral rehearsal of Sibelius' Second Symphony. The conductor, Gaetano Delogu, had just arrived, full of vim, eager to begin. I and my novices sat out of sight at the side. Delogu conducted the first 11 notes of the opening movement – those lilting, swaying, repeating chords for strings which lead to the puckish theme for oboes

– and stopped dead. He conducted them again. And again. And again. And again, each time slightly differently, with terse explanations of what he wanted and was not being given. Pulsations, accents, crescendi, diminuendi, phrase-ends, balances, and the echoing extensions were gradually and rigorously worked out.

Only then, when Delogu was finally satisfied, could the performance proceed. Would this demanding Sicilian conductor have done the same to a professional orchestra? Hard to say – though easy, perhaps, to imagine the orchestra's thoughts if he had. Yet this, whatever everybody felt about it, was a revelation in how to handle a great symphony's opening bars. Delogu recognised, as the players as yet probably did not, that on these liquid phrases the entire structure of the first movement floated. He was surely right to devote so much immediate attention to them. The result was an object lesson – for a critic as much as for the players – in time vitally spent.

Would it have been a performance fit for the Edinburgh Festival as well as for an Usher Hall programme at New Year? Or would it have seemed to the Festival authorities to be simply 'very creditable'? That there is a pecking order among youth orchestras for concerts at great international festivals is perhaps inevitable. At present in Edinburgh the Gustav Mahler Jugendorchester, created by Claudio Abbado, heads the list, and the performance of *Parsifal* at the Festival Theatre in 2002 showed why. Its depth, weight, and beauty of string tone proved astonishing, yet some mishaps in the wind during the prelude revealed that it was not foolproof. That this is now the Rolls-Royce of youth orchestras, however, seemed unquestionable.

But does quality alone justify these players becoming a Festival fixture, or is it the ailing Abbado's conducting that matters? Either way it is an awe-inspiring achievement, which Brian McMaster, the Festival's director, is doubtless anxious to sustain as long as he can. It should not, however, preclude an occasional appearance by NYOS, just as a concert by the Berlin Philharmonic should not stand in the way of one by the RSNO. Yet NYOS has not been invited to perform at the Edinburgh Festival since 1988, though it was heard playing Stravinsky's *Petrushka* and a new work by Gordon McPherson at the Amsterdam Concertgebouw in the summer of 2002. Though no orchestra, not even one from the host country, has an automatic right to perform at the

Edinburgh Festival, it is time, I would say, for NYOS to be featured again.

Conrad Wilson is author of books on Scottish Opera and the Royal Scottish National Orchestra and of the authorised biography of Sir Alexander Gibson. Born in Edinburgh, he was music critic of *The Scotsman* from 1964 until 1991 and since then has written regularly for *The Herald*. He was the Edinburgh Festival's programme editor for 16 years, and lectures on opera at Glasgow University.

FOUR

Pennies, Politics

VIII

Finding the Funds

In the first 25 years of NYOS, there have been two principal changes in its finances. First, the tremendous increase in the activities undertaken (see Chapter Five) has made necessary a comparable increase in funding. Second, there has been a significant change in funding from only a few sources, including one major sponsor, to funding from literally hundreds of sources. The management of funding so diverse and unpredictable requires a combination of courage and competence – or call it carefully controlled housekeeping – on the part of both staff and council. In this respect NYOS has been most fortunate.

Total expenditure in the 15 months represented in the first NYOS accounts was £54,581. In the accounts for 2001, total expenditure was £592,854 (inflation is not taken into account in any of these figures). In 1979–80 there were 17 sources of NYOS income, whereas in 2002 there were nearly 170, plus more than 160 paying Friends. These sources are in addition to the contributions made by councils, local and regional – support from which is considered below as part of funding from the public purse.

Throughout history the arts have benefited from patronage of one kind or another. Samuel Johnson described a patron as 'commonly a wretch, who supports with insolence, and is paid with flattery'. Arts organisations of today have little reason to speak thus harshly of their sponsors. The trouble is, simply, finding and keeping them. The late 1970s have been described as the beginning of the age of sponsorship.[1] NYOS began with the benefit of generous and – for 16 years – sustained sponsorship from BP. By 1984, NYOS accounts showed BP providing 33.4 per cent of total NYOS income. Other sponsorship in that year brought the total percentage from sponsors to 34.8, the peak percentage figure in 25 years from this category. Twice in the quarter century sponsorship income has fallen below 15 per cent of income.

Sponsors' reasons (see Chapter Three) are deep and various. Attitudes and personnel change from year to year – in sponsoring companies, also in trusts, arts quangos and government departments. By the mid-1990s NYOS had to look around for new sources of support, but alas in the company of many other arts bodies, this partly because government funding of the arts in general was being reduced.

Between 1992 and 1998 government funding of the arts was reduced in real terms by £13 million while business sponsorship for the arts grew by £28 million to a total of £95 million.[2] Robin Wight, chairman of the Association for Business Sponsorship of the Arts (ABSA), wrote in 1998 that business involvement in the arts was very thinly rooted: only two of the top ten sponsors of a decade previously were still among the top ten sponsors in 1998. The fundamental difficulty, he said, was that the constituencies of government and business (i.e. taxpayers and shareholders) were not properly persuaded of the value of art to either of them.[3] Some experienced seekers-after-funds might, on the other hand, be inclined to argue that, so far as allocation of sponsorship is concerned, the chairmen, chief executives or PR personnel in companies have much more clout than shareholders have; and further, there is little evidence that politicians consult their constituents about the arts.

By 2001 Jane Patterson-Todd, head of development at the Barbican, London, was reported as suggesting that the age of sponsor miracles was now passing. She wrote: 'Corporate sponsorship is a dying market. Too many people are chasing the same corporations. There are only a certain number out there and they have finite pots.'[4]

Corporate sponsorship of the arts in Britain, however, was by 2001 said to be worth £150 million a year.[5] At the time of the Arts & Business (formerly ABSA) 2002 awards ceremony in Scotland the figures showed a fall (from £16 million to £8 million) in business support for the arts in the previous two years. Worthy charitable causes, sport and commercial TV were attracting more sponsorship funding. At the same time, fortunately, sponsorship in kind was increasing.

By 2002, the search for an ample share of the still available funds had become a most exacting challenge for NYOS. A recurring question for any such organisation is how much staff time and salary investment is required for, and then justified by, the sponsorship funding achieved, in large or small amounts. To what extent can staff, whatever their titles or qualifications – in marketing, development or public affairs – be expected to deliver more funding year after year? How many council members of an arts organisation should be chosen – or can be found – because of their own wealth or their rewarding contacts? To what extent should NYOS council approval of proposed innovations or expansions depend on the likelihood of sponsorship?

The total amount of sponsorship seldom reflects the effort expended upon securing it. No company or person is obliged to enter the sponsor partnership, nor to stay within it for ever. Music and youth are clearly deserving causes, though classical music may not be the first preference of all youth. How much exposure, or even mention, does a sponsoring company gain, in proportion to its funding, from a youth orchestra in comparison, say, with sport? In 1982 when generous BP support made possible the NYOS Viking Tour to Orkney, the Faroes and Scandinavia, BBC Scotland sent a film crew to make a documentary of this impressive and expensive tour. But the film, otherwise a creditable production, made scarcely a mention of BP. The BBC has since then accepted more readily the obligation to acknowledge sponsorship given to arts bodies whose work is broadcast.

There is difficulty in arguing that a youth orchestra can, in media terms, merit repeated and extended exposure in comparison with a competitive sport or game – soccer, snooker, golf or whatever. These not only have their matches broadcast on radio and TV but are also the subject of extended discussion and reporting. Invariably, in studio or outdoors, for sport there is displayed on TV a background of prominent corporate logos. Ties and cravats worn by young orchestral players, even with a sponsor's banner above the platform, may not be seen to have impact at all comparable with a logo-bedecked soccer strip which thousands of children wish to be seen wearing. In the mid-1980s some high-powered sponsors, including BP, were known to be considering a transfer of funds to football; then there were some rowdy incidents at matches and the sponsors thought again. It's an ill wind that blows nobody any good but it is not within the power or the wish of arts organisers to ensure recurring bouts of soccer hooliganism. Nor, for that matter, does an organisation like NYOS wish to face the problems of a football club whose survival may depend on the renewal of broadcasting rights. New problems of competition for sponsorship have, however, been created for arts companies by sports organisations which have till recently been well funded by tobacco companies and must now try to draw from the finite pots as described above.

The best time for presenting arguments to sponsors, donors, trusts is not usually when these have already decided to transfer their support. BP was especially proud to be in at the beginning of NYOS. But arts organisations do not come into being every year, nor can they dream up novel projects year after year. Novel projects present their own problems: pump-priming for the new idea pre-supposes early finality of funding, after which other funding must be sought. All sponsorship contracts set time limits, eventually not extended. Tomorrow, to fresh woods and funding pastures new, where scores of other fund-raisers have already set up camp, have picked the rosy fruits and reaped harvests for competing worthy causes.

It goes without saying that the beneficiaries of sponsorship wish to persuade the sponsors that the money is being well spent. Sponsors' criteria for judging a music concert by young players are likely to be different from those for a soccer match. The performance itself may not be the sole or the main benefit involved. Much may depend on who is invited to a concert by the arts organisation and by the sponsor. Networking may be of the essence for both sponsor and sponsored. The possibility of creating a NYOS Trust was discussed over a period of years. The eventual setting-up of the NYOS Endowment Trust is credited to an eminent Edinburgh solicitor who was invited to several NYOS receptions and then, it is believed, advised a wealthy client that NYOS was a deserving cause, meriting inclusion in a will. The trust has, *deo gratias*, benefited from a number of bequests; *deo volente*, it will continue to do so. May many wealthy Scots go to meet their Maker confident in the knowledge that angels will play their harps for them.

FINDING THE FUNDS

Sometimes a sponsor generously entertains pre-concert, mid-concert and post-concert. Such occasions can be greatly pleasurable, sometimes they are problematic. For a start, who is invited? If the event has involved 120 young players – these must be bussed back to their beds, often with an early start and a long journey the following day – should a crowd of adults celebrate the success of the concert without any young players being present? If some, how many, how chosen? Are exhausted conductor and soloist expected to appear, before or after obligatory speeches? If the Royal Patron is present and wishes, most laudably, to seek the company primarily of the players, then who from the assembled guests should also be introduced? Do sponsors' staff and/or eminent guests expect priority?

Sponsoring companies – happily sometimes sponsors do not come singly – have their own conflicting priorities. Some may see concert and reception simply as a means of entertaining deserving staff from the locality. This may mean that no prestigious guests, potential sponsors or people of political influence are present. Some of the sponsor's deserving staff may never before have attended an orchestral concert. Or, as happened when Glasgow celebrated its year as City of Culture, chosen staff may move day by day in festive spirit from one sponsored event and reception to another, punch-drunk, as it were, with unfamiliar culture. Thus, one dares to hope, new audiences may be won: a long-term prospect. Audiences do matter.

Whereas professional orchestras depend on box office for nearly 70 per cent of income (as indicated in a 1991 survey[6]) youth orchestras and youth organisations apparently draw under 20 per cent of income from box office takings. NYOS has only occasionally drawn more than ten per cent of its income from box office. But such statistics can be misleading: the more corporate members and sponsors' guests there are (payment for or by these does not usually come via the box office) the less one can easily relate actual box office figures to audience numbers. Most important in relating total NYOS income to box office is the fact that the more training courses and educational services are provided by NYOS, the less relevant box office takings become. Concert performances are not the principal end product of all NYOS activities.

A significant element in NYOS funding has come from the public purse, that is from local authorities, the Scottish Arts Council, the education department of succeeding Scottish governments, or sometimes Lottery grants, the level of which sometimes affects the income from other pockets of the public purse. The Foundation for Sport and the Arts allotted a grant of £50,000 towards the purchase of the NYOS office premises at 13 Somerset Place, Glasgow.

In the late 1970s both the SED and the SAC swithered about funding the new NYOS (see Chapter Two). The SAC said it could fund the commissioning of new works but at that time it had no precedent for funding children and amateurs. NYOS answered that it employed a number of professionals – as tutors, conductors and soloists. By 1980 the SAC was deciding that it would channel funds to NYOS. After three years most of the monies from the public purse came to NYOS not from the SAC but from the SED or its retitled and reconstituted successors (while the SAC continued to fund such projects as jazz and the commissioning of new works). This arrangement continued until 2000 when major funding reverted to the SAC. Music in general has become very demanding on public funds, so is a body like NYOS at a disadvantage if, for its now widely varied activities, it is adding to the already onerous sum-total of the SAC's allocation to music, in 2002 at least 40 per cent of SAC funds? Such allocation has in turn to be represented by the SAC in its bids for music funding within an overall submission to Comprehensive Spending Reviews undertaken by the Scottish Executive, which determines the National Cultural Strategy. In September 2002 the review indicated standstill funding for the SAC in 2003–4.[7] In the same month the *Herald*[8] published the results of a survey. On page one it declared:

Holyrood has failed us badly, says arts world
Poll reveals disillusion
Devolution has done little or nothing for the arts in Scotland, according to an unprecedented survey of the nation's cultural leaders.

An exclusive poll of more than 100 leading art organisations, artists, cultural commentators and academics has found nearly two-thirds believe government does not care enough about art and culture.

The poll [. . .] found that 63 per cent of those questioned felt devolution had failed to improve conditions for creative people, while more than 70 per cent said the Executive had not given culture the importance it deserved.

NYOS must perform a puzzling series of balancing acts. It has had to define and redefine itself to suit the immediate purpose – the immediate purpose, of course, being the search for funds. The puzzle is made difficult when government departments and ministers change their titles and functions and categories of interest. Ministers in charge of both the arts and tourism may tend to favour those arts that tourists are thought to associate with Scotland (though in Festival time the proliferation in Edinburgh city centre of pipers of variable proficiency may not be entirely helpful to the tourist cause). Education has been partnered, now with tourism, now with sport, now with culture: perhaps the daftest alliance has been the Westminster creation of a department for culture, media and sport (including licensing laws).[9] How many in-trays can be squeezed onto one ministerial desk?

In 2002 James Boyle, SAC chairman, arguing that the arts should be at the centre of education policy, called for substantial additional funding for 'this kind of artistic mission'.[10] His plea was followed by advertisements in which the SAC and Fife Council together sought to recruit Fife Cultural Champions in Schools' Initiative (FCCISI); these champions to be 'motivated and dynamic individuals who will work together to enhance, extend and link both curricular and out of school time cultural (Heritage and Expressive Arts) learning opportunities for children and young people in Fife'.

The temporary senior cultural co-ordinator would, hopefully, be

> an excellent communicator and people manager/motivator [. . .] able to work to strict deadlines and possess a degree in a related educational and/or cultural/arts discipline or community education (i.e. visual arts and design, the performance arts – drama, music, dance, ICT, moving image and multi-media media, 'heritage, folklore and language').[11]

Within education, how does or should music compete against art and design, drama, and sport (the categories used in the SOED Working

Paper 6[12]) or as in a 1976 SED Report[13] with Dance, or as, in the above, against ICT or whatever is embraced by 'heritage, folklore and language'? Over the centuries music has been seen by many as pre-eminent in the arts ('the greatest good that mortals know'[14]) but don't try using that argument in a room full of competing representatives from the other related educational and/or cultural/arts disciplines – and sport. Public funds come from identified compartments or departments; arguments and justifications have to be presented and adjusted to fit the compartments – and present company. NYOS staff and/or council members must, in turn, acquire the skills for negotiation with those who allocate public funds. Many commercial sponsors are easier to tackle.

The first money to NYOS from either SAC or SED came from the SAC in 1981: it was a welcome £10,000, 11.6 per cent of NYOS' income. By the time the funding channel was moved over to the SED, in 1984, the sum was up at £19,200, 18.5 per cent. By 1989 the SED was giving £28,000 (at 11.2 per cent the same as BP was giving). In the 1994 NYOS accounts the education department was giving £45,000 (again the same as BP at 11.8 per cent). In the accounts for 2000, the figure was £65,000, 10.8 per cent (but now no BP). In the 2001 accounts public money was coming from the SAC, at £69,375, 11.5 per cent. All this time the work of NYOS had been increasing, with its other ensembles and other initiatives.

Local authority (district and regional) contributions are difficult to detail precisely, for an appreciable amount of local council funding comes through the payment per capita of course fees for individual students, but at varying levels and paid direct to students. Some councils have paid a nominal lump sum in respect of student support. Funding direct to NYOS from local authorities has varied between 0.3 per cent and 8.7 per cent. Income from course fees was shown in 1980 accounts as £10,976 (18.9 per cent); by 2001 it was £145,463 (24.1 per cent), this with other ensembles included.

One NYOS principle has remained through the years: no student who justifies a place is prevented from attending by shortage of money. There are few cases where the student is funded 100 per cent by NYOS, perhaps one or two each year and restricted to older students, the reason for this being that, while local authorities will support, in part or whole, applications from school pupils, anyone who has left full-time education is invariably turned down for even partial funding. Aidan Thomson, a member of NYOS from 1991 to 1998 and eventually leader of the orchestra, wrote in the 1998 summer programme:

> Students simply do not have the money nowadays [. . .] But it is not just students who are suffering financially. Free instrumental tuition for school pupils at local authority level is increasingly becoming a thing of the past [. . .] Contrary to popular (and populist) belief, music tuition and music courses are not a subsidised luxury for middle-class children.

A NYOS Bursary Fund was set up by NYOS in 1980 with a donation from the Carnegie United Kingdom Trust. Other funds have been provided by generous donors and some of these have at times helped towards course fees. The total paid out by NYOS in support of fees has tended to exceed the total available from bursary funds. The cost as shown in NYOS 2001 accounts for bursary payments was some £20,000.

The fact is that a truly economic fee for NYOS courses would be astronomical. For the first NYOS course, council decided to make the fee marginally lower than that charged by NYOGB: since when NYOS has gone its own way. The calculation of appropriate fee level has little relationship to budgeted costs and has to be based on what is thought reasonable, with NYOS finding the rest, as best it can, from sponsors and other sources. Student fees could be said to be paying for accommodation, tuition and some overhead costs. Travel supplements, which may be required for summer courses, are more easily calculated: in 2001–02 they formed just under ten per cent of the total fee income from all courses.

Total income to NYOS in its first accounts was nearly £60,000. After ten years it was £215,635. In 2000 it was £589,891. Staff costs and expenses began at nearly £16,000, 29.2 per cent of expenditure. In 1990 they were £44,552, 29.4 per cent. In 2000 they were £235,664, 38.1 per cent. Such accounting categories may be misleading. Audition costs in 1980 were shown as £2,082 (3.8 per cent); in 1990 they were £3,583 (2.4 per cent), and in 2000 they were £12,746 (2.1 per cent). But these do not include the major staff contribution (by director and administrator) to the work of auditioning. Also, as suggested elsewhere, the loss of a major sponsor makes necessary an increase in staff activity, probably numbers, in order to advance the work of fund-raising. Since the early 1990s this has been largely in the hands of Lesley Paterson, as public affairs administrator. (At the start, NYOS considered the possibility of employing outside professional fundraisers, but couldn't afford them.)

In the early years NYOS council had oversight of the one symphony orchestra, engaging more than 100 young players each year. Today the organisation gives performing orchestral experience each year to about four times that number in at least six ensembles. In most respects, not least in expenditure and effort, the orchestra which has the title of the National Youth Orchestra of Scotland still holds pre-eminence as the flagship of the extended enterprise.

Last but not least: in calculations of income and expenditure, of pre-eminence and priority, for an organisation like NYOS one category is too often and too easily overlooked or taken for granted. That is the contribution made by parents, a contribution which is incalculable and cannot appear in annual accounts. In 1976 the Scottish education department acknowledged rather lamely (see Chapter One) that much depended on the chance coincidence of a gifted child having enlightened school teachers as well as enlightened and supportive parents.[15] The situation has changed little in 30 years. Parents often provide the initial stimulus, while their continuing support is essential. Many parents pay – have to pay – for instrumental tuition. They pay for instruments, for uniforms, for all manner of transport – in addition to NYOS travel supplements. Parents come to concerts as a paying audience. They bring brothers and sisters, aunts and uncles, grannies and grandpas. In all, a family backing for their offspring. When NYOS was celebrating its 100th concert in 1991, BP and NYOS council invited parents to a thank-you reception so that some measure of appreciation could be expressed. Appreciation must be repeatedly expressed: it is the appreciation owed by any structure to its foundation.

IX

NYO of Scotland

The first NYOS concert was part of the 1979 Falkirk Tryst (see Chapter Two). In the concert programme the local provost, Alexander Crawford, recalled that the drove roads of old had led to Falkirk, where at the Tryst the culture and folklore of the Gael was heard in counterpoint with the sound of the traditional fiddle, Highland bagpipe and Lallans ballad. The aims of the Tryst, he wrote, were:

> to recreate the spirit of bygone years as artistes and musicians from all over the world 'travel the drove roads' to the ancient site of Callendar Park. With their coming, Falkirk audiences have the opportunity to see and hear a range of talented performers embracing many different and interesting cultures.

On Sunday, 12 August 1979 Falkirk Tryst extended a warm but undeniably wet welcome to 115 talented performers from all over Scotland. On Monday, 13 these young pioneers of the new NYOS moved on to Aberdeen.

At the end of the NYOS concert in Aberdeen's Music Hall, the packed audience gave Scotland's new orchestra a prolonged standing ovation. From the gallery an anonymous enthusiast exclaimed, 'We've done it!' In a year when many lamented the fact that devolution had not yet come to Scotland, was this a sign that at least one kind of devolution had been achieved?

NYOS has carried the National title lightly. It has reason to claim that it has served Scotland well, as well as and in much the same way as the National Youth Orchestra of Great Britain served Britain for 30 years before NYOS began. Ruth Railton, founder of the NYOGB, had to cope with a lot of opposition in her early years with the orchestra, but she records no questioning of the Great Britain in the NYOGB title.[1] NYOS, on the other hand, has at times been challenged by people with diverse Scottish preoccupations and commitments: is NYOS, they have asked, proving itself Scottish, sufficiently Scottish, for instance, to merit a good share of monies from the Scottish public purse? Does it commission or play a meaningful proportion of works by Scottish composers?

The questioning may also imply that, while some arts in Scotland are traditionally Scottish, symphony orchestras are not, and for the most part these orchestras perform a kind of music, designated as classical or (sometimes dismissively) as continental, which is not. The questions may also come with a hint that not very many Scots actually care about this kind of music – it isn't music of the people – and that those who do care about it are well-heeled, elitist snobs who don't need public funding.

The numbers argument is often based less on a passion for proportional representation than on class distinction – from which Scotland suffers its share. The tendency was apparent, though ironically, at a meeting of a local authority education committee in the 1980s when a councillor challenged NYOS representatives who had been invited to attend and to justify their plea that NYOS members' course fees should be paid by the council. Pointing to a list of young applicants, the councillor protested that many of them came from an area where parents must surely have ample resources for the payment of fees. It was pointed out to him that the parents were in the catchment area – some had deliberately moved there – of a school specifically designated and funded by the same local council as a specialist music school. How best does one learn to appreciate the movement and the variety of party political attitudes?

The numbers argument is sometimes deployed by those who suggest that what most people, especially the young, really care about is pop music, which happily manages for the most part to be commercially self-supporting. But since it is so popular, they say, let public funds be allocated to young Scots with pop ambitions and potential not yet realised. Iain Hamilton, composer and academic, likened rock concerts and musicals to spectator sports.[2] Most music-makers – pop, rock, jazz, classical or otherwise – do welcome spectators. They all seek an audience, preferably large. (According to research by the UK Arts Council, the proportion of under-24s attending concerts of classical music fell from 8.4 to 4 per cent between 1999 and 2002.[3] No figures available on audiences for pop music.)

The world of classical music is, presumably, indebted to Classic FM, which has won a new and large radio audience for the more melodic items of the genre. This may in part account for the mindset of the large door-keeping gent stationed at the entrance to an Edinburgh Princes Street music store: when asked where classical CDs could be purchased, he proclaimed: 'All easy listening upstairs'! Fine, so long as easiness does not threaten excellence, nor threaten music which may make exacting demands of players and audience.

As for questions about Scotland's traditional music, classical orchestral music is not so long or so deeply established in Scotland that at the beginning of the twenty-first century it should seek to be defined as traditionally Scottish or Celtic, not in the way that many people (in line with the aims of the Falkirk Tryst) define as traditional the music of the fiddle, the Highland bagpipes, the clarsach, the bothy ballad, the Lallans ballad, the work song, the folk song, or the reel. The RSAMD, affirming its Scottishness, has been offering to an American college a course in the use of these traditional Scottish instruments.[4] In turn, the Scottish Arts Council,[5] the tourist organisation VisitScotland[6] and the Saltire Society[7] have all sought to proclaim their support for Scottish traditional music and culture. As of course they should.

For many years up to the middle of the twentieth century, however, the music that many Scots knew best – or well – was church music. From the time of St Columba (he sang 'like a melodious lion') there has been a recurring and strong relationship between church music and the people, the music often drawing markedly on native melodies. A contributor to *The Times* in 2002 invoked the Catechism of the Catholic Church: 'the musical tradition of the universal church is a treasure of inestimable value, greater than that of any other art'.[8] Some of the best historic traditions in the arts transcend and challenge national boundaries.

Burns, sometimes preoccupied with national identity, contributed much to the corpus of Scottish song, at the same time affirming the psalm tune as a well-established part of Scottish music. He also pointed to a suspect import:

> They chant their artless notes in simple guise,
> They tune their hearts, by far the noblest aim;
> Perhaps Dundee's wild-warbling measures rise,
> Or plaintive Martyrs, worthy of the name,
> Or noble Elgin beets the heavenward flame,
> The sweetest far of Scotia's holy lays;
> Compared with these, Italian trills are tame.[9]

A century later, for Andrew Carnegie one way of showing appropriately Scottish support for his native land was by giving generous grants towards the purchase of countless church organs.

The music of Scotland has, over the years, become increasingly multifarious in its styles, its sources, its strengths, its locations and its devotees. In the course of the twentieth century, by means of music hall, broadcasting and records, there were established the couthy choruses, the tartan-bedecked fiddle and accordion kitsch which many Scots have acclaimed proudly as their own and have promoted for tourist and ex-pat consumption. Of comparatively recent origin, such music perhaps merits the title of 'continuing traditional musical culture of Scotland'.[10] Whatever – it's all good fun. Easy listening!

Now, in the twenty-first century, must be added the music from continents afar. In July 2002 the Scottish executive culture minister launched a drive to involve more people from ethnic communities in Scotland's arts. About 1.25 per cent of Scotland's population, *The Scotsman* reported, has an ethnic-minority background. The SOED Working Paper No. 6, Expressive Arts 5–14, had already advised in 1991:

> Society is becoming ever more culturally complex and diverse. In ever-expanding multi-cultural communities it is vital to use the

experience provided within expressive arts to give pupils opportunities to learn about, share, respond to and understand other forms of cultural expression. Through this pupils will extend their understanding of the multicultural nature of society. All regional and national cultures should be regarded from the outset as being of equal status and worthy of equal respect.[11]

Not having a markedly ethnic connotation and not benefiting from this kind of cultural or political embrace, classical music falls both within and beyond ethnic categories, but presumably meriting equal respect.

Resistance to music that has been categorised as classical is by no means recent in Scotland. We are told (as reflected in Burns' lines above) that such resistance developed alongside a Scottish identity crisis two centuries ago, this after both French and Italian influences had over many years effected significant changes in song, dance and instrumental music in Scotland.[12] Today's renewal of Scottish identity has revived some of the old questions, but in a rather different context. By the beginning of 2002 the new Scottish executive was attempting to codify Scottish culture and to set out a cultural strategy.

In 2003 Glasgow University's music department is reported to be introducing a course in contemporary music culture. The course will look 'at virtually any type of music today's students experience in Glasgow – within reason, of course'. [13] What are the musical bounds of reason? Glasgow, perhaps more than any other British city, has been influenced by – as it has greatly influenced – the culture of America. Like all the rest of Scotland, Glasgow sang the songs and danced to the music – it also absorbed much of the language – of the early films from Hollywood. By means of films and records, of radio and television, people of the twentieth century could listen to the music of the world. There developed, between Britain and America, a two-way interchange of popular music, including jazz. In one sense, jazz has been lucky in being seen frequently, by politicians, sponsors and many others, as so unarguably popular – and of the people – that it merits funding priority. John Drummond, who first introduced jazz to the Edinburgh International Festival, offers a personal view: he recalls a meeting with John Birt, then BBC director-general, who pulled up the sleeves of the Armani jacket, and talked about only one thing – the refuge, always, of the uninterested: 'Do we,' he asked, 'do enough about jazz?' I explained that whatever we did would never be enough, since no audience in the world is more divided in what it likes.[14]

Scotland itself is divided in what it likes. Who would have it otherwise? Let diversity prosper!

In the twentieth century, at much the same time as jazz and swing were gaining popularity in Scotland, orchestral activities were slowly, perhaps less obtrusively, gaining momentum. From its founding in 1891 the Scottish National Orchestra was part-time until 1950. Meantime the first full-time professional orchestra in Scotland, a BBC studio orchestra of 35 players, was formed in 1935.[15] The Edinburgh International Festival, founded in 1947, did much to stimulate interest in orchestral music. The first Scottish conductor of the Scottish National Orchestra, Alexander Gibson, was appointed in 1959. After which, professional opera and ballet companies were established in Scotland, and sought their shares of public support.

The historian H. A. L. Fisher wrote in his *History of Europe*: 'A small handful of remarkable Scots and Englishmen, fewer than would be required for a football match, succeeded by their ingenuity in transforming the economic life of the country.'[16]

A similarly small handful of men transformed the musical life of Scotland in the latter half of the twentieth century. Gibson, as principal conductor and artistic director of the SNO (strongly supported by Robert Ponsonby), then as artistic director of the newly formed Scottish Opera (in partnership with Peter Hemmings and Robin Orr) augmented the audiences for music in Scotland. These men enhanced and enriched the making of music. In *Musica Nova*, along with Professor Frederick Rimmer, Gibson gave great encouragement to Scottish composers. It was Gibson who then offered the lifeline that ensured the survival of the NYOS project when in 1977 he authorised David Richardson to tell a rather despondent meeting in Edinburgh that the SNO would be willing to provide administrative support for the early years of a national youth orchestra. Alexander Gibson was a major determinant of that musical climate of Scotland which made it possible and timely for NYOS to be created.

NYO of Scotland

Scottish culture has rarely been static. Scots have influenced the thoughts and feelings of peoples around the world. In turn Scots have been inspired and informed by so much that has come to them from lands near and distant. Scottish artists, writers and musicians, having digested and absorbed what is around them, recreate the language or idioms of their own and other communities. They have stimulated people in Scotland to look and listen afresh and anew. In its first quarter century NYOS has been a beneficiary of, and has contributed to, a developing Scottish culture. The concert programmes of NYOS, Camerata Scotland, NYJOS, and NCOS (see appendices) give some indication of the extent to which the National Youth Orchestras of Scotland have reflected or influenced Scotland's music. The first NYOS programme began with the popular Hamish McCunn overture, *The Land of the Mountain and the Flood.* The 2003 summer NYOS programme begins with the overture, *The Comedy of Errors* by the little-known Scottish composer Cecil Coles.[17] John McLeod, Edward McGuire, Thomas Wilson and other contemporary Scottish composers have been given prominence in NYOS programmes over the years.

In all of its courses NYOS has engaged the professional skills of a large number of tutors, and has thereby contributed to the musical skills of many hundreds of young instrumentalists, as to the quality of instrumental teaching in Scotland and the quality of performance in many orchestras, amateur and professional. It has unashamedly made excellence one of its principal goals, alongside the enjoyment of music by as many people as will come to play it or hear it. NYOS has taken great music to parts of Scotland hitherto unvisited by symphony orchestras. It has taken young Scottish musicians to countries near and far – ambassadors for Scotland and for music, a language 'which ideally ignores the boundaries set up by the imperfections of the human species'.[18]

NOTES

CHAPTER ONE
1. *Scotsman*, 4 March 1980
2. *Times*, 8 June 2002, Obituary of Dee Dee Ramone
3. Quoted in Foreword of SED (1976) *Gifted Young Musicians and Dancers*. HMSO, London
4. *Ibid.*
5. SED Curriculum Paper 16 (1978) 'Music in Scottish Schools'. HMSO, London
6. *TES* Scotland, 18 June, 1976
7. Railton, R. (1992) *Daring to Excel*. Secker & Warburg, London

CHAPTER TWO
1. Railton, R. (1992) *Daring to Excel*. Secker & Warburg, London
2. *Herald*, 15 August 1979
3. *Guardian*, 15 August 1979
4. *Scotsman*, 15 August 1979

CHAPTER THREE
1. Drummond, J. (2000) *Tainted by Experience*. Faber & Faber, London
2. *Ibid.*
3. *Times*, 29 August 2002
4. Railton, R. (1992) *Daring to Excel*. Secker & Warburg, London
5. Drummond, J. (2000) *Tainted by Experience*. Faber & Faber, London
6. *Brabants Dagblad*, 8 August 1988
7. *Scotsman*, 4 August 1980
8. *TES* Scotland, 22 August 1980
9. *Scotsman*, 24 July 2002

Notes

10. Railton, R. (1992) *Daring to Excel*. Secker & Warburg, London
11. *Ibid.*
12. Glennie, E. (1990) *Good Vibrations*. Hutchinson, London
13. *Ibid.*
14. *Scotsman*, 4 January 2002, Kenneth Wilson

CHAPTER FIVE
1. Railton, R. (1992) *Daring to Excel*. Secker & Warburg, London
2. *TES* Scotland, April 2000
3. *Herald*, 13 April 2002
4. Expressive Arts 5–14 SOED Working Paper No. 6. (1991) HMSO pp. 19 and 57

CHAPTER SIX
1. *TES* Scotland, 25 January 2002
2. Expressive Arts 5–14
3. *Ibid.* p. 69
4. *Ibid.* p. 31
5. *Ibid.* p. 35
6. *Ibid.* p. 59
7. *Instrumental Instruction in Schools* issued through the Association of Music Advisers in Scotland
8. *Ibid.*
9. *TES* Scotland, 10 June 1994

CHAPTER EIGHT
1. Drummond, J. (2000) *Tainted by Experience*. Faber & Faber, London
2. *Spectator*, 25 July 1998
3. *Spectator*, 25 July 1998
4. *Spectator*, 17 November 2001
5. *Spectator*, 17 November 2001
6. 'Funding of Orchestras in the UK', Ernst & Young
7. *Scotsman*, 27 September 2002
8. *Herald*, 30 September 2002
9. *Times*, 3 October 2002
10. Expressive Arts 5–14
11. *Scotsman*, 11 October 2002
12. *Scotsman*, 21 May 2002
13. Gifted Young Musicians and Dancers
14. 'A Song for St Cecilia's Day', Joseph Addison
15. Gifted Young Musicians and Dancers

CHAPTER NINE
1. Railton, R. (1992) *Daring to Excel*. Secker & Warburg, London
2. MacLean, C. (ed.) (1979) *Crown & Thistle*. Scottish Academic Press, Edinburgh
3. *Times*, 29 August 2002
4. *Herald*, 20 June 2002

5. *Scotsman*, 24 July 2002

6. *Scotsman*, 25 July 2002

7. *Scotsman*, 27 July 2002

8. Quoted in *The Times*, 27 April 2002 by Antony Bye, editor of *The Musical Times*

9. Robert Burns, 'The Cotter's Saturday Night'

10. *Scotsman*, 27 July 2002

11. Expressive Arts 5–14

12. Purser, J. (2000) *Tainted by Experience*. Faber & Faber, London

13. *Scotsman*, 4 March 2002

14. Drummond, J. (2000) *Tainted by Experience*. Faber & Faber, London

15. Purser, J. (1992) *Scotland's Music*. Mainstream, Edinburgh

16. Fisher, H. A. L. (1936) *History of Europe*. Arnold, London

17. Cecil Coles. Born in Tongland, Kirkcudbright in 1888, educated in Edinburgh, a colleague and friend of Gustav Holst, Coles died of wounds near the Somme in April 1918.

18. Ebert, P. in MacLean, C. (ed.) (1979) *Crown & Thistle*. Scottish Academic Press, Edinburgh

APPENDIX 1

The National Youth Orchestra of Scotland: Works Performed

SUMMER, 1979
MacCunn, *The Land of the Mountain and the Flood*
Mozart, Clarinet Concerto
Tchaikovsky, Fantasy Overture: *Romeo and Juliet*
Respighi, *Pines of Rome*
Venues: Big Top, Callendar Park, Falkirk; Caird Hall, Dundee; Music Hall, Aberdeen
Conductor: Nicholas Braithwaite
Soloist: Janet Hilton

WINTER, 1979–80
Glinka, *Russlan and Ludmilla* Overture
Shostakovich, Cello Concerto No. 2
John McLeod, *The Shostakovich Connection* (conducted by composer)
Borodin, Symphony No. 2
Venues: Usher Hall, Edinburgh; City Hall, Glasgow
Conductor: Edward Downes
Soloist: Marius May

SUMMER, 1980
Wagner, *The Flying Dutchman* Overture
Elgar, *Enigma Variations*
Mozart, Oboe Concerto
Ravel, *Daphnis and Chloe*, Suite No. 2
Venues: Hilltop Centre, Sullom Voe; Anderson High School, Lerwick; Phoenix Cinema, Kirkwall

Wagner, *The Flying Dutchman* Overture
Maxwell Davies, *Five Klee Pictures*
Elgar, *Enigma Variations*
Strauss, Horn Concert No. 1
Ravel, *Daphnis and Chloe*, Suite 2
Venues: Phoenix Cinema, Kirkwall; High School, Thurso; Eden Court Theatre, Inverness

Nurturing Talent

Conductor: Nicholas Kraemer
Soloists: Elizabeth Fyfe (oboe); Frank Lloyd (horn)

WINTER 1980–1
Dvorak, Carnival Overture
Mendelssohn, Violin Concerto
Roussel, Symphony No. 3
R. Strauss, *Till Eulenspiegel*
Venues: City Hall, Glasgow; Usher Hall, Edinburgh; City Hall, Perth
Conductor: Norman Del Mar
Soloist: Nigel Kennedy

SUMMER, 1981
Prokofiev, scenes from *Romeo and Juliet*
Mozart, Flute and Harp Concerto K299
Stravinsky, *The Rite of Spring*
Venues: Academy Hall, Dumfries; Caird Hall, Dundee; Music Hall, Aberdeen
Conductor: Nicholas Braithwaite
Soloists: John Grant (flute); Saida De Lyon (harp)

WINTER, 1981–2
Walton, *Partita*
Mozart, *Sinfonia Concertante*, K364
Rachmaninov, Symphony No. 2
Venues: Playhouse, Edinburgh; Pavilion, Ayr; City Hall, Glasgow
Conductor: Sir Alexander Gibson
Soloists: Pamela Redman (violin); Susan Young (viola)

SUMMER, 1982
Berlioz, *Le Carnaval Romain* Overture
Beethoven, *Egmont* Overture
Elgar, *Sea Pictures*
Tchaikovsky, Violin Concerto
John McLeod, *The Gokstad Ship*
Debussy, *La Mer*
Venues: Grammar School Kirkwall (two concerts); Itrottarholl, Torshavn, Faroe
   Islands; Grieghallen, Bergen, Norway; Konserthus, Oslo, Norway;
   Konserthus, Goteborg, Sweden; Tivoli Concert Hall, Copenhagen, Denmark
Conductor: Nicholas Braithwaite
Soloists: Christine Cairns (soprano); Nigel Kennedy (violin)

WINTER, 1982–3
R. Strauss, *Don Juan*
Grieg, Piano Concerto
John McLeod, *The Gokstad Ship* (conducted by composer)
Mussorgsky/Ravel, *Pictures at an Exhibition*
Venues: City Hall, Glasgow; Usher Hall, Edinburgh
Conductor: Sir Charles Groves
Soloist: Peter Evans

APPENDIX 1

SUMMER, 1983
Berlioz, *Les Francs Juges* Overture
Prokofiev, Piano Concerto No. 3
Alan Fernie, A Scots Folk Song Suite
Nielsen, Symphony No. 4, *The Inextinguishable*
Mendelssohn, Hebrides Overture
Webern, Six Pieces, Op. 6
Ravel, *Scheherazade*
Venues: Nicolson Institute, Stornoway; Eden Court Theatre, Inverness; Festival Theatre, Pitlochry; Music Hall, Aberdeen; Usher Hall, Edinburgh (Edinburgh International Festival)
Conductors: Christopher Adey; Sir Alexander Gibson (Usher Hall)
Soloists: Murray MacLachlan (piano); Isobel Buchanan (soprano)

WINTER, 1983–4
Alan Fernie, A Scots Folk Song Suite (conducted by composer)
Rodrigo, *Concierto de Aranjuez*
Janacek, *Sinfonietta*
Rimsky–Korsakov, *Sheherazade*
Venues: City Hall, Glasgow; Usher Hall, Edinburgh; Pavilion, Ayr
Conductor: Norman Del Mar
Soloist: Paul Galbraith (guitar)

SUMMER, 1984
Brahms, Variations on the St Anthony Chorale
Ravel, *Tzigane*
Arutunian, Trumpet Concerto
Mahler, Symphony No. 1
Venues: Grammar School, Kirkwall (two concerts); High School, Thurso; Inverness Cathedral, Inverness; Music Hall, Aberdeen; Community Centre, Westray
Conductor: Nicholas Braithwaite
Soloists: Claire Docherty (violin); Christopher Bradley (trumpet)

WINTER, 1984–5
Beethoven, Overture *Leonora* No. 3
Prokofiev, Violin Concerto No. 2
Rachmaninov, Symphony No. 3
Venues: Usher Hall, Edinburgh; City Hall, Glasgow
Conductor: Christopher Adey
Soloist: Erich Gruenberg

SUMMER, 1985
Kabalevsky, Overture *Colas Breugnon*
John McCabe, *Tuning*
Tchaikovsky, Piano Concerto No. 1
Dvorak, Cello Concerto in B minor
Strauss, *Ein Heldenleben*
Venues: Casinotheater, s'Hertogenbosch; Zeltingen, West Germany; Markplatz,

Bonn, West Germany; Wiltz Sports Hall, Luxembourg; Albert Hall, Stirling; (concerts in Kerkrade, Trier and Ripon cancelled)
Conductor: Nicholas Braithwaite
Soloists: Walter Civitareale (piano); Raphael Wallfisch (cello)

WINTER, 1985–6
Britten, *The Young Person's Guide to the Orchestra*
Beethoven, Piano Concerto No. 4 in G
John McCabe, *Tuning* (conducted by composer)
Stravinsky, *Petrouchka*
Venues: Usher Hall, Edinburgh; City Hall, Glasgow
Conductor: Christopher Adey
Soloist: John Lill

SUMMER, 1986
Berlioz, Overture *Le Corsaire*
Hamilton, *Aurora*
Brahms, Violin Concerto
Rachmaninov, *Rhapsody on a Theme of Paganini*
Sibelius, Symphony No. 2

Encores
Sibelius, *Karelia* Suite
Nielsen, *An Imaginary Journey to the Faroes*
Venues: Clickimin Centre, Lerwick; Sports Hall, Runavik, Faroe Islands; Teacher Training College, Torshavn; Konserthus, Stavanger; Music Hall, Aberdeen; Eden Court Theatre, Inverness
Conductor: Sir Alexander Gibson
Soloists: Krzysztof Smietana (violin); Murray McLachlan (piano)

WINTER, 1986–7
Wagner, *Die Meistersinger Prelude*
Poulenc, *Gloria* (SNO Junior and Youth Choruses with the Amicorum)
Holst, *The Planets* (with a section of the SNO Youth Chorus)
Venues: City Hall, Glasgow; Usher Hall, Edinburgh
Conductor: Nicholas Braithwaite
Soloist: Patricia MacMahon (soprano), SNO Junior Chorus

SUMMER, 1987
John McLeod, Percussion Concerto (conducted by composer)
Gershwin, *An American in Paris*
Tchaikovsky, Symphony No. 4
Arnold, Overture *Tam O'Shanter*
Walton, Viola Concerto
Roy Sinclair, *Intrada* (winning work of 1987 BP Young Scottish Composers Competition)
Venues: Nicolson Institute, Stornoway; High School, Thurso; Eden Court Theatre, Inverness; Festival Theatre, Pitlochry; Music Hall, Aberdeen
Conductor: Christopher Adey

Appendix 1

Soloists: Evelyn Glennie (percussion); Paul Coletti (viola)

WINTER, 1987–8
Strauss, *Der Rosenkavalier Suite*, Op. 59
John McLeod, Percussion Concerto (conducted by composer)
Dvorak, Symphony No. 9 in E minor, Op. 95 (New World)
Venues: Usher Hall, Edinburgh; City Hall, Glasgow
Conductor: Yan Pascal Tortelier
Soloist: Evelyn Glennie

SUMMER, 1988
Programme A
Arnold, Overture *Tam O'Shanter*
Rachmaninov, Piano Concerto No. 3
Shostakovich, Symphony No. 5
Venues: Casinotheater, s'Hertogenbosch; Caird Hall, Dundee; City Hall,
    Glasgow (Glasgow Festival of British Youth Orchestras); Royal Albert Hall,
    London; (BBC Henry Wood Promenade Concert)
Conductor: James Loughran
Soloist: John Lill

Programme B
Berio, *La Ritirata Notturna Di Madrid*
Rachmaninov, Piano Concerto No. 3
Musgrave, Concerto for Orchestra
Respighi, *Pines of Rome*
Venues: De Reehorst, Ede, Netherlands; Usher Hall, Edinburgh (Edinburgh
    International Festival)
Conductor: James Loughran
Soloist: John Lill

WINTER, 1988–9
Rossini, Overture *Semiramide*
Bruch, Violin Concerto No. 1
Mahler, Symphony No. 1 in D
Venues: Usher Hall, Edinburgh; City Hall, Glasgow; Loreburn Hall, Dumfries
Conductor: Diego Masson
Soloist: Lorraine McAslan

SUMMER, 1989
Berlioz, Overture *Benvenuto Cellini*
Britten, *Four Sea Interludes* – Peter Grimes
Strauss, Oboe Concerto
Sibelius, Violin Concerto
Brahms, Symphony No. 2 in D
Stravinsky, *The Rite of Spring*
Venues: Phoenix Cinema, Kirkwall (two concerts); The High School, Thurso;
    Eden Court Theatre, Inverness; City Hall, Glasgow; Music Hall, Aberdeen
Conductor: Sian Edwards

NURTURING TALENT

Soloists: Douglas Boyd (oboe); Jennifer Wion (violin)

WINTER, 1989–90
David Horne, *Light, Emerging . . .*
Wagner, *Wesendonk Lieder*
Berlioz, *Symphonie Fantastique*
Venues: Usher Hall, Edinburgh; City Hall, Glasgow
Conductor: Matthias Bamert
Soloist: Linda Finnie (mezzo soprano)

SUMMER, 1990
Wagner, *Prelude and Liebestod – Tristan And Isolde*
Brahms, Violin Concerto in D
Edward McGuire, *A Glasgow Symphony*
Weber, Overture *Der Freischutz*
Mozart, Bassoon Concerto
Elgar, Symphony No. 1
Venues: City Hall, Glasgow; Stevenson Hall, RSAMD, Glasgow; Casinotheater,
    s'Hertogenbosch; Concertgebouw, Amsterdam; De Doelen Hall, Rotterdam
Conductor: James Loughran
Soloists: Sungsic Yang (violin); Kim Walker (bassoon)

WINTER, 1990–1
Verdi, Overture *La Forza Del Destino*
Beethoven, Piano Concerto No. 1
Tchaikovsky, Ballet Suite: *Swan Lake*
Tchaikovsky, *Francesca Da Rimini*
Venues: Usher Hall, Edinburgh; Royal Concert Hall, Glasgow; Music Hall,
    Aberdeen
Conductor: Jun'ichi Hirokami
Soloist: Michael Roll

SUMMER, 1991
Brahms, Academic Festival Overture
Britten, *Symphonia Da Requiem*
Vaughan Williams, *London Symphony*
Rachmaninov, Piano Concerto No. 2
Prokofiev, Symphony No. 5
Venues: Lochaber High School, Fort William; Royal Concert Hall, Glasgow;
    Philharmonic Hall, Liverpool; Les Invalides, Paris; Eglises, St Denis, Paris;
    The Madeleine, Paris; Music Hall, Aberdeen
Conductor: Sergei Vlasov
Soloist: Peter Katin

WINTER, 1991–2
Rossini, Overture *The Thieving Magpie*
Jolivet, Percussion Concerto
Mahler, Symphony No. 5
Venues: Royal Concert Hall, Glasgow; Usher Hall, Edinburgh; Music Hall, Aberdeen

Appendix 1

Conductor: Takuo Yuasa
Soloist: Evelyn Glennie

SUMMER, 1992
Saeverud, *Ballad Of Revolt*
Walton, *Henry V* Suite
Elgar, Cello Concerto
Britten, *The Young Person's Guide to the Orchestra*
Ravel, *Daphnis and Chloe* Suite No. 2
*Berlioz, *Requiem*
Venues: Royal Concert Hall, Glasgow; Bodø Kulthurhus, Norway; *Bodø
    Cathedral, Norway (three performances); Grieghallen, Bergen, Norway;
    Konserthus, Stavanger, Norway
Conductor: Louis Fremaux
Soloist: Juliane Von Hahn

WINTER, 1992–3
Glinka, Overture *Russlan and Ludmilla*
Brahms, Piano Concerto No. 1 Op. 15
Strauss, *Tod Und Verklarung* Op. 24
Venues: Usher Hall, Edinburgh; Royal Concert Hall, Glasgow; Music Hall,
    Aberdeen
Conductor: Roland Kieft
Soloist: John Lill

SUMMER, 1993
Shostakovich, Festival Overture
Thomas Wilson, Violin Concerto
Holst, *Planets* Suite
Venues: Music Hall, Aberdeen; Pitlochry Festival Theatre; Royal Concert Hall,
    Glasgow; Symphony Hall, Birmingham; Royal Albert Hall, London (BBC
    Henry Wood Promenade Concert)
Conductor: Christopher Seaman
Soloist: Ernst Kovacic

WINTER, 1993–4
Bernstein, *Fancy Free*
Lalo, Cello Concerto in D
Tchaikovsky, Symphony No. 2
Venues: Usher Hall, Edinburgh; Royal Concert Hall, Glasgow
Conductor: Sian Edwards
Soloist: Raphael Wallfisch

SUMMER, 1994
Stravinsky, *The Fairy's Kiss* – Divertimento
Ibert, Flute Concerto
Tchaikovsky, Symphony No. 4 (Stirling, Rotterdam, Amsterdam)
Mahler, Symphony No. 4 (Glasgow, s'Hertogenbosch, Birmingham)

NURTURING TALENT

Encore
Johann Strauss, *Thunder and Lightning Polka*
Venues: macRobert Arts Centre, Stirling; Royal Concert Hall, Glasgow; The
Province House, s'Hertogenbosch; De Doelen, Rotterdam; Concertgebouw,
Amsterdam; Symphony Hall, Birmingham
Conductor: Jun'ichi Hirokami
Soloists: Lisa Milne (soprano) Glasgow & Birmingham; Willemijn Van Gent
(soprano) s'Hertogenbosch; William Bennett (flute)

WINTER, 1994–5
R. Strauss, *Don Juan*
Dvorak, *Scherzo Capriccioso*
Elgar, *Sea Pictures*
Brahms, Symphony No. 1
Venues: Usher Hall, Edinburgh; Royal Concert Hall, Glasgow; Music Hall,
Aberdeen
Conductor: Bramwell Tovey
Soloist: Jane Irwin (mezzo soprano)

SUMMER, 1995
Samuel Barber, Essay No. 2 Op. 17
Dave Heath, *African Sunrise–Manhattan Rave*
Sibelius, Symphony No. 1
Venues: Phoenix Cinema, Kirkwall; High School, Thurso; Marco's An Aird, Fort
William; Royal Concert Hall, Glasgow; Town Hall, Elgin; Music Hall,
Aberdeen
Conductor: Stephen Barlow
Soloist: Evelyn Glennie

WINTER, 1995–6
Prokofiev, *Love of Three Oranges* Suite
Szymanowski, Violin Concerto No. 1 Op. 35
Rachmaninov, Symphony No. 2
Venues: Usher Hall, Edinburgh; Royal Concert Hall, Glasgow
Conductor: Takuo Yuasa
Soloist: Raphael Oleg

SUMMER, 1996
Elgar, *In the South*
R. Strauss, *Four Last Songs*
Shostakovich, Symphony No. 10
Venues: Royal Concert Hall, Nottingham; Casinotheatre, s'Hertogenbosch;
Concertgebouw, Amsterdam; Symphony Hall, Birmingham; Royal Concert
Hall, Glasgow
Conductor: Ole Schmidt
Soloist: Roberta Alexander

WINTER, 1996–7
Smetana, *Blanik: Ma Vlast*

APPENDIX 1

Khachaturian, Violin Concerto
Sibelius, Symphony No. 2
Venues: Usher Hall, Edinburgh; Royal Concert Hall, Glasgow
Conductor: Gaetano Delogu
Soloist: Kai Gleusteen

SUMMER, 1997
Holst, *The Perfect Fool*
Musgrave, Horn Concerto
Elgar, Symphony No. 1
Venues: macRobert Arts Centre, Stirling; Music Hall, Aberdeen; Royal Concert
    Hall, Glasgow; Usher Hall, Edinburgh
Conductor: Bramwell Tovey
Soloist: Michael Thompson

WINTER, 1997–8
Poul Ruders, *Concerto in Pieces*
Beethoven, Piano Concerto No. 5 'Emperor'
Mussorgsky–Ravel, *Pictures at an Exhibition*
Venues: Festival Theatre, Edinburgh; Royal Concert Hall, Glasgow
Conductor: James Loughran
Soloist: John Lill

SUMMER, 1998
Rory Boyle, *Capriccio*
Prokofiev, Piano Concerto No. 3
Berlioz, *Symphonie Fantastique*
Venues: s'Hertogenbosch, Holland; Concertgebouw, Amsterdam; Royal Albert
    Hall, London (BBC Henry Wood Promenade Concert); Symphony Hall,
    Birmingham; Royal Concert Hall, Glasgow
Conductor: Jun'ichi Hirokami
Soloist: Peter Donohoe

WINTER, 1998–9
Berlioz, *Carnaval Romain*
Sibelius, Violin Concerto
Bartok, Concerto for Orchestra
Venues: Royal Concert Hall, Glasgow; Festival Theatre, Edinburgh
Conductor: Nicolae Moldoveanu
Soloist: Dong-Suk Kang

SUMMER, 1999
Wagner, *Dei Meistersinger*, Prelude
Tchaikovsky, Violin Concerto
Ravel, *Daphnis and Chloe*, Suites 1 and 2
Venues: Westmorland Hall, Kendal; Symphony Hall, Birmingham; Philharmonic
    Hall, Liverpool; Royal Concert Hall, Glasgow; Music Hall, Aberdeen
Conductor: Takuo Yuasa
Soloist: Tasmin Little

Nurturing Talent

WINTER, 1999–2000
Edward Harper, *Etude*
Bernstein, 'Symphonic Dances' from *West Side Story*
Ian Whyte, 'The Devil's Finale' from *Donald of the Burthens*
Prokofiev, *Romeo and Juliet*, Suites 1 and 2
Strauss, *Der Rosenkavalier* Suite
Venues: Festival Theatre, Edinburgh; Royal Concert Hall, Glasgow; Ryan Centre, Stranraer
Conductors: Iain Sutherland; Garry Walker (Prokofiev)

SUMMER, 2000
Geddes, Symphony No. 3
Schnittke, Cello Concerto No. 1
Elgar, *Enigma Variations*
Venues: Casinotheatre, s'Hertogenbosch; Konzerthaus, Berlin; Royal Concert Hall, Glasgow
Conductor: Sian Edwards
Soloist: Alexander Baillie

WINTER, 2000–1
John McLeod, *The Sun Dances*
Grieg, Piano Concerto Op. 16 in A minor
Tchaikovsky, Symphony No. 4 Op. 36 in F minor
Venues: Usher Hall, Edinburgh; Royal Concert Hall, Glasgow
Conductor: Takuo Yuasa
Soloist: Steven Osborne

SUMMER, 2001
Sibelius, *Finlandia* Op. 26
Brahms, Violin Concerto Op. 77 in D
Shostakovich, Symphony 5 Op. 47 in D minor
Venues: Nevis Centre, Fort William; Royal Concert Hall, Glasgow; Music Hall, Aberdeen; Westmorland Hall, Kendal
Conductor: Petter Sundkvist
Soloist: Janine Jansen

WINTER, 2001–2
Dvorak, Carnival Overture, Op. 92
Bruch, Violin Concerto No. 1 in G minor, Op. 26
Mahler, Symphony No. 1 in D
Venues: Usher Hall, Edinburgh; Royal Concert Hall, Glasgow
Conductor: Garry Walker
Soloist: Dong Suk-Kang

SUMMER, 2002
Gordon McPherson, *South*
Schumann, Piano Concerto
Stravinsky, *Petrouchka*
Venues: Pickaquoy Centre, Kirkwall; Eden Court Theatre, Inverness; Royal

Concert Hall, Glasgow; Westmorland Hall, Kendal; Symphony Hall, Birmingham; Concertgebouw, Amsterdam
Conductor: Nicolae Moldoveanu
Soloist: Andreas Boyde

WINTER, 2002–3
Stravinsky, *The Song of the Nightingale*
Szymanowski, Violin Concerto No. 1
Tchaikovsky, Symphony No. 6
Venues: Usher Hall, Edinburgh; Royal Concert Hall, Glasgow
Conductor: Sian Edwards
Soloist: Mihaela Martin

SUMMER, 2003
Coles, Overture, *The Comedy Of Errors*
Beamish, Trumpet Concerto
Elgar, Symphony No. 2
Venues: Royal Concert Hall, Glasgow; Royal Albert Hall, London (BBC Henry Wood Promenade Concert); Salzau, Schleswig Holstein Festival; Konzerthaus, Berlin
Conductor: Martyn Brabbins
Soloist: Håkan Hardenberger

APPENDIX 2

Camerata Scotland: Works Performed

APRIL 1992
Haydn, Symphony No. 44 in E minor
Ravel, *Pavane Pour Une Infante Defunte*
Edward McGuire, *Symphonies of Trains*
Schubert, Symphony No. 1 in D
Venues: Stevenson Hall, RSAMD, Glasgow; Queen's Hall, Edinburgh
Conductor: William Conway

APRIL 1993
Mozart, Symphony No. 29
Thomas Wilson, *St Kentigern* Suite
Beethoven, Symphony No. 2 in D
Venues: Music Hall, Aberdeen; Stevenson Hall, RSAMD, Glasgow
Conductor: William Conway

Nurturing Talent

AUGUST 1993
Mozart, Overture *Cosi Fan Tutti*
Edward Harper, *Fiddler of the Reels*
Beethoven, Symphony No. 2
Venues: World Youth Orchestra Festival; Toyohashi; Ohta; Ichikawa, Nagoya
    Japan
Conductor: William Conway

DECEMBER 1993
Mozart, Symphony No. 29
Beethoven, Symphony No. 2 in D
Venues: Stevenson Hall, RSAMD, Glasgow (Recording: City Hall, Glasgow)
Conductor: William Conway

APRIL 1994
Mozart, *Eine Kleine Nachtmusik*
Schubert, Symphony No. 5
Mozart, Overture *Marriage of Figaro*
Haydn, Symphony No. 103
Venues: Stevenson Hall, Glasgow (LASMO Staffa Music Award); Tait Hall,
    Kelso; Marco's An Aird, Fort William
Conductor: Gerard Korsten

AUGUST 1994
Haydn, Symphony No. 96
Sibelius, *Pelleas et Melisande*
Aulius Sallinen, *Variations for Orchestra*
Stravinsky, *Pulcinella* Suite

Encore
Edward Harper, *Fiddler of the Reels*
Venues: Stevenson Hall, RSAMD, Glasgow; Central Hall Tollcross, Edinburgh
Conductor: William Conway

APRIL 1995
Rossini, *Tancredi Overture*
Edward Harper, *Fantasia V: Passacaglia*
Mozart, Violin Concerto No. 3 K216
Beethoven, Symphony No. 1 in C
Venues: Victoria Hall, Helensburgh; Queen's Hall, Edinburgh (LASMO Staffa
    Music Award); Stevenson Hall, RSAMD, Glasgow
Conductor/Soloist: Ernst Kovacic

SUMMER 1995
Rossini, Overture *The Italian Girl in Algiers*
Haydn, Trumpet Concerto
Francaix, *L'horloge De Flore*
*Edward Harper, *Fiddler of the Reels*
Vaughan Williams, *Lark Ascending*

APPENDIX 2

Haydn, *Sinfonia Concertante*
Edward McGuire, *The Fiddler's Farewell*
Venues: Music Hall, Aberdeen
*Conductor*s: Julian Clayton; *Edward Harper
(*Soloists*: representing Skene Award winners of past 20 years)

SUMMER 1995
Rossini, Overture *The Italian Girl in Algiers*
Stravinsky, *Dumbarton Oaks*
Haydn, Trumpet Concerto
Beethoven, Symphony No. 4
Venues: Victoria Hall, Campbelltown; Bonar Hall, Dundee; Rothes Hall, Glenrothes
Conductor: William Conway
Soloist: Tracey Redfern

APRIL 1996
Stravinsky, Pulcinella Suite
Dvorak, Czech Suite
Venues: Stevenson Hall, RSAMD, Glasgow (LASMO Staffa Music Award)
Conductor: William Conway

John Lewis Partnership Concert
Rossini, Overture *The Italian Girl in Algiers*
Berlioz, *Les Nuits D'ete* (*Soloist*: Hester Dam)
Beethoven, Symphony No. 4
Venues: St Giles' Cathedral, Edinburgh
Conductor: William Conway
Soloist: Hester Dam

John Lewis Partnership Concert
Haydn, Symphony No. 96
Mozart, *Exultate Jubilate*
Harper, *Fiddler of the Reels*
Dvorak, Czech Suite
Venues: St Michael's Parish Church, Linlithgow
Conductor: William Conway
Soloist: Felicity Hammond

John Lewis Partnership Concert
Sibelius, *Pellas & Melisande* Suite
Haydn, Trumpet Concerto
Stravinsky, *Pulcinella*
McGuire, *Fiddler's Farewell*
Venues: St Mary's Parish Church, Haddington
Conductor: William Conway
Soloist: Tracey Redfern

Nurturing Talent

AUGUST 1996
Beethoven, *Egmont* Overture
Maxwell Davies, *Into the Labyrinth*
Mendelssohn, Symphony No. 3 'Scottish'
Venues: Central Hall, York; Maltings Snape
Conductor: William Conway
Soloist: Neil Mackie (tenor)

APRIL 1997
Thomson, Overture *Hermann*
J. S. Bach, *St Matthew Passion – 'Erbarme Dich'*
Thomson, *Three Lieder*
Mendelssohn, Symphony No. 3 'Scottish'
Venues: Queen's Hall, Edinburgh (LASMO Staffa Music Award); Stevenson
    Hall, RSAMD, Glasgow; (Recording, Greyfriars Kirk, Edinburgh)
Conductor: William Conway
Soloist: Colette Ruddy (mezzo soprano)

JULY/AUGUST 1997
Mendelssohn, Hebrides Overture
David Horne, *Flicker*
Matthew Hindson, *Rave–Elation*
Beethoven, Symphony No. 7
Venues: Concert Hall, Sydney Opera House; Town Hall, Melbourne;
    Woolstores, Geelong; Town Hall, Adelaide; Winthrop Hall, Perth; Barbican
    Hall, London; Symphony Hall, Birmingham; Bridgewater Hall, Manchester;
    Royal Concert Hall, Glasgow; Music Hall, Aberdeen
Conductor: Matthias Bamert
(tour in collaboration with Camerata Australia)

APRIL 1998
Rossini, Overture *The Silken Ladder*
Mendelssohn, Violin Concerto
Honneger, *Pastorale D'ete*
Haydn, Symphony No. 94 *Surprise*
Venues: Queen's Hall, Edinburgh (LASMO Staffa Music Award); Tait Hall,
    Kelso; Bonar Hall, Dundee; Rothes Hall, Glenrothes
Conductor: Roland Keift
Soloist: Kai Gleusteen

AUGUST 1998
Shostakovich, Symphony for Strings and Woodwind
Britten, *Les Illuminations*
Mozart, Symphony No. 35 *Haffner*
Macmillan, *Tryst*
Saint-Saëns, Cello Concerto No. 1
Dvorak, Czech Suite
Venues: Champagne Congrès, Reims; St Mary-In-The-Castle, Hastings; St
    James's, Piccadilly, London; Stevenson Hall, RSAMD, Glasgow

APPENDIX 2

Conductor: William Conway

SEPTEMBER 1998
Jan Sandstrøm, *A Scottish Story*
Tchaikovsky, Serenade for Strings
Venues: Assembly Rooms, Wick (Northlands Festival)
Conductor: Malin Broman
Soloist: Christian Lindberg

MARCH/APRIL 1999
Malcolm Arnold, Serenade for Small Orchestra
Mozart, Symphony No. 31 *Paris*
Venues: Stevenson Hall, RSAMD, Glasgow (LASMO Staffa Music Award)
Conductor: Roland Melia

John Lewis Partnership Concerts
Rossini Il, S*ignor Bruschino* Overture
Malcolm Arnold, Serenade for Small Orchestra
Dvorak, Romance for Solo Violin
Leroy Anderson, *Fiddle Faddle*
Mozart, *The Marriage of Figaro* Overture
Saint-Saëns, Introduction and *Rondo Capriccioso*
Mozart, Symphony No. 31 *Paris*
McGuire, *Fiddler's Farewell*
Venues: Greyfriars Church, Edinburgh; St Mary's, Haddington; Dunfermline Abbey
Conductor: Roland Melia
Soloist: Daniel Bell

AUGUST 1999
Mozart, Symphony No. 29
Mozart, Violin Concerto K216
Beethoven, Symphony No. 2
Venues: Stevenson Hall, RSAMD, Glasgow; Concertgebouw, Amsterdam; Casinotheatre, s'Hertogenbosch
Conductor: William Conway
Soloists: Nicolaj Znaider, Concertgebouw; Daniel Bell, Glasgow & s'Hertogenbosch

APRIL 2000
Faure, *Masques et Bergamasques*
Poulenc, *Sinfonietta*
Schubert, Symphony No. 3
Venues: Tait Hall, Kelso; Rothes Hall, Glenrothes; Matt Thomson Concert Hall, RSAMD Glasgow (LASMO Staffa Music Award)
Conductor: Christopher Adey

SEPTEMBER 2000
Vivaldi, *The Four Seasons* (Winter)
Greig, Holberg Suite

Greig, *Norwegian Dances*
Holst, St Paul's Suite
Venues: St Mary's Cathedral, Edinburgh
Conductor: Kai Gleusteen

APRIL 2001
Schubert, Overture *Rosamunde*
Saint-Saëns, Piano Concerto No. 2 Op. 22 in G minor
Mozart, Overture *The Magic Flute*
Mendelssohn, Symphony No. 4 (Italian)
Venues: Rothes Hall, Glenrothes; Ryan Centre, Stranraer; Royal Concert Hall,
    Glasgow (Recording RSAMD, Glasgow)
Conductor: Gerard Korsten
Soloist: Peter Seivewright

SEPTEMBER 2001
Bach, Suite No. 2 in B minor for Flute and Strings
Vivaldi, *The Four Seasons*
Tchaikovsky, *Souvenir of Florence*
Venues: St Andrew's in the Square, Glasgow
Conductor: Daniel Rowland

APRIL 2002
Beethoven, *Coriolanus* Overture Op. 62
Honegger, Symphony No. 2 for Strings and Trumpet
Brahms, Serenade No. 1 Op. 1 in D major
Venues: Queen's Cross Church, Aberdeen; Bonar Hall, Dundee; Royal Concert
    Hall, Glasgow; Nevis Centre, Fort William
Conductor: Christoph Mueller

AUGUST 2002
Mendelssohn, Hebrides Overture
Sibelius, *Pelleas and Melisande*
Bach, Concerto for two Violins and Strings
Schubert, Symphony No. 1 in D
Venues: Music Hall, Aberdeen; Beach Ballroom, Aberdeen; Westmorland Hall,
    Kendal
Conductor: William Conway
Soloists: Daniel Rowland; Donald Grant

APRIL 2003
Venues: Webster Theatre, Arbroath; Royal Concert Hall, Glasgow; Corran
    Halls, Oban
Conductor: Garry Walker

APPENDIX 3

The National Youth Jazz Orchestra of Scotland: Works Performed

JULY 1996
Jones, 'Kids are Pretty People'
Coltrane, arranged Mantooth, 'Moment's Notice'
Kupka & Castillo, arranged Taylor, 'Attitude Dance'
Michael, 'Blues for Big Joe'
Gourlay, 'Persephone'
Michael, 'Stroma Samba'
Venue: macRobert Arts Centre, Stirling
Director: Richard Michael

JULY 1997
Traditional, arranged Oddo, 'John Brown's Other Body'
Howard, arranged Taylor, 'Fly Me to the Moon'
Berry, arranged Mintzer, 'Christopher Columbus'
Moten & Moten, arranged Blair, 'Moten Swing'
Kupka & Castillo, arranged Taylor, 'Attitude Dance'
Venue: macRobert Arts Centre, Stirling
Director: Richard Michael

JULY 1998
Yeoh, 'Quiet Freedom' Part 1
Ellington, Tizol & Mills, arranged Lopeman, 'Caravan'
Brecker, arranged Taylor, 'Skunk Funk'
Jones, 'Kids are Pretty People'
Coltrane, arranged Mantooth, 'Moment's Notice'
Venue: macRobert Arts Centre, Stirling
Directors: Richard Michael; Nikki Yeoh

OCTOBER 1998
Yeoh, 'Quiet Freedom' Part 1
Ellington, arranged Stone, 'I Let a Song Go Out of My Heart'
Coltrane, arranged Mantooth, 'Moment's Notice'
Watson, arranged Watson, 'Ms B.C.'
Stone, 'Caught in the Current'

Venue: the Lemon Tree, Aberdeen
Directors: Eddie Severn; Nikki Yeoh

MARCH 1999
Yeoh, 'Quiet Freedom' Part 1
Brecker, arranged Taylor, 'Skunk Funk'
Severn, 'Saturn'
Ellington & Mills, arranged Holmes, 'It Don't Mean a Thing'
Venue: Eden Court Theatre, Inverness
Directors: Eddie Severn; Nikki Yeoh

JULY 1999
Yeoh, 'Quiet Freedom' Parts 1 & 2
Berry, 'Samba Ya Bamba'
Arguelles, 'Ha Bloody Ha'
Severn, 'Saturn'
Venues: macRobert Arts Centre, Stirling; Old Fruitmarket, Glasgow; the Hub,
   Edinburgh (Edinburgh Jazz Festival)
Directors: Eddie Severn; Nikki Yeoh

JANUARY 2000
Coltrane, arranged Mantooth, 'Moment's Notice'
Arguelles, 'Skull View'
Arguelles, 'Such Sweet Moments'
Severn, Edinburgh Suite
Parker, arranged Holmes, 'Ornithology'
Venue: the Lemon Tree, Aberdeen
Director: Eddie Severn

JULY 2000
Arguelles, 'Ha Bloody Ha'
Arguelles, 'Such Sweet Moments'
Arguelles, 'Skull View'
Severn, 'Saturn'
Caribe, 'Pluto'
Coltrane, arranged Mantooth, 'Moment's Notice'
Bancroft, 'Papa Joe'
Venue: macRobert Arts Centre, Stirling; the Hub, Edinburgh (Edinburgh Jazz
   Festival)
Directors: Eddie Severn; Laura MacDonald

JANUARY 2001
Bancroft, 'The Battle of Camp Bongo'
Bancroft, 'Sleepyhead'
Arguelles, 'Skull View'
Severn, Edinburgh Suite
Hancock, 'Watermelon Man'
Campbell, 'Rizla Man'
Cairney, new work – untitled

Appendix 3

Venue: the Lemon Tree, Aberdeen
Directors: Tom Bancroft; Laura MacDonald; Mario Caribe

JULY 2001
Bancroft, 'Fear is not the Key'
MacDonald, 'Back Green Odyssey'
Golson, arranged Purcell, 'Killer Joe'
Cairney, new work – untitled
Venue: macRobert Arts Centre, Stirling
Directors: Simon Purcell; Laura MacDonald; Tom Bancroft

JULY 2001
Bancroft, 'Fear is not the Key'
MacDonald, 'Back Green Odyssey'
Lyall, 'Little Suite for Jazz Orchestra'
Rae, 'Roots to Fruits'
Caribe, 'Many Voices, Bright Lights'
Ellington, 'Cottontail'
Ellington, Tizol & Mills, arranged Lopeman, 'Caravan'
Venue: the Hub, Edinburgh
Directors: Laura MacDonald; Tom Bancroft

FEBRUARY 2002
Ellington, Tizol & Mills, arranged Lopeman, 'Caravan'
Bancroft, 'Fear is not the Key'
Venue: the Lemon Tree, Aberdeen
Directors: Laura MacDonald; Tom Bancroft

MAY 2002
Rae, 'Roots to Fruits'
Ellington, 'Never no Lament (Don't Get Around Much Anymore)'
Lyall, 'Little Suite for Jazz Orchestra'
Caribe, 'Many Faces Bright Lights'
Ellington, arranged Berger & Wallarab, 'Cottontail'
MacDonald, 'Back Green Odyssey'
Parker, 'Now's the Time' (NYJOS Quintet)
Bancroft, 'Fear is not the Key'
Venue: The Corn Exchange, Haddington
Directors: Laura MacDonald; Tom Bancroft

JULY 2002
S. Bancroft, 'Dreams of a Prairie Sea'
Wells, 'The Man I Love/Of thee I Sing'
Edmonstone, 'The Poplar/That time again'
O'Donnell, 'I'd Love To . . .'
P. Bancroft, 'Colour Theory'
Venue: the Hub, Edinburgh (Edinburgh Jazz Festival)
Directors: Laura MacDonald; Tom Bancroft

FEBRUARY 2003
Edmonstone, 'The Poplar/That time again'
Caribe, 'Many Voices, Bright Lights'
Wells, 'The Man I Love/Of Thee I Sing'
Oakland, arranged Mantooth, 'I'll Take Romance'
Rogers, arranged Stone, 'It Might as well be Spring'
Gershwin, arranged MacDonald, 'I Loves you Porgy'
Rogers, arranged MacDonald, 'Lonely Goatherd'
Ellington, Tizol & Mills, arranged MacDonald, 'Caravan'
Venue: the Lemon Tree, Aberdeen
Director: Laura MacDonald & Mario Caribe

APPENDIX 4

The National Children's Orchestra Of Scotland: Works Performed

APRIL 1996
Arnold, Little Suite
Boieldieu, Overture *The Calif of Baghdad*
Holst, St Paul's Suite (1st Movement)
Venue: Merchiston Castle School, Edinburgh
Directors: James Durrant; Lewis Morrison

APRIL 1997
Arnold, Anniversary Overture
William McGibbon, Sonata in G
Mussorgsky, *Night on the Bare Mountain*
Kenneth Leighton, Dance Suite No. 2
Venue: Queen's Hall, Edinburgh
Director: James Durrant

APRIL 1998
Arnold, Little Suite No. 2
Vivaldi, *The Four Seasons* (Spring)
Edward McGuire, Scottish Dances
Massenet, *Le Cid* Ballet Suite
Venue: Queen's Hall, Edinburgh
Director: James Durrant
Soloist: Nicola Benedetti

Appendix 4

APRIL 1999
Grieg, Three Orchestra Pieces from *Sigurd Jorsalfron*
Hallgrimsoon, *Daydreams in Numbers*
Britten, *Soirées Musicales*
Chabrier, Scherzo-Valse Suite Pastorale
Venue: Queen's Hall, Edinburgh
Director: Nigel Murray

APRIL 2000
Leighton, Dance Suite No. 1
Tchaikovsky, Serenade for Strings (3rd Movement)
Delius, *Sleigh Ride*
Bizet, *Carmen* Suite
Venue: Queen's Hall, Edinburgh
Director: Nigel Murray

APRIL 2001
Dvorak, Slavonic Dance in G minor Op. 46 No. 8
Bach, Concerto for Four Pianos
John Maxwell, *Geddes Dances at Threave*
Grieg, *In the Hall of the Mountain King*
Offenbach, *Overture Orpheus in the Underworld*
Venue: Royal Concert Hall, Glasgow
Director: Nigel Murray
Soloists: Louisa Laing; Eugenie Younger; Isla Pitkethly; Mary Erskine

APRIL 2002
Brahms, Academic Festival Overture
Lutoslawski, Little Suite
Dvorak, Romance for Violin and Orchestra
Massenet, *Le Cid* Ballet Music
Venue: Royal Concert Hall, Glasgow
Director: Julian Clayton
Soloist: Nicola Benedetti

APRIL 2003
Walton Crown Imperial, Coronation March
Beethoven, Romance No. 2 in F for violin and orchestra
Maw, *Summer Dances*
Tchaikovsky, *Marche Slave*
Venue: Royal Concert Hall, Glasgow
Director: Julian Clayton

APPENDIX 5

National Youth Orchestras of Scotland: Works Commissionsed

John McLeod	*The Gokstad Ship*	NYOS SC 1982
Alan Fernie	A Scots Folk Song Suite	NYOS SC 1983
John McCabe	*Tuning*	NYOS SC 1985
John McLeod	Percussion Concerto	NYOS SC 1987
David Horne	*Light, emerging . . .*	NYOS WC 1989/90
Edward McGuire	*A Glasgow Symphony*	NYOS SC 1990
Edward McGuire	*Symphonies of Trains*	CAMERATA Spring 1992
Edward Harper	*Fiddler of the Reels*	CAMERATA Summer 1993
Thomas Wilson	Violin Concerto	NYOS SC 1993
Dave Heath	*African Sunrise–Manhattan Rave*	NYOS SC 1995
David Horne	*Flicker*	CAMERATA Summer 1997
Rory Boyle	*Capriccio*	NYOS SC 1998
Nikki Yeoh	'Quiet Freedom'	NYJOS Summer 1998 and 1999
Edward Harper	*Etude for Orchestra*	NYOS WC 1999/2000
John Maxwell Geddes	Symphony No. 3	NYOS SC 2000
John McLeod	*The Sun Dances*	NYOS WC 2000/01
Laura MacDonald	'Back Green Odysses'	NYJOS Summer 2001
Tom Bancroft	'Fear is not the Key'	NYJOS Summer 2001
Mario Caribe	'Many Voices, Bright Lights'	NYJOS Summer 2001
Chick Lyall	Little Suite for Jazz Orchestra	NYJOS Summer 2001
John Rae	'Roots to Fruits'	NYJOS Summer 2001
Gordon McPherson	*South*	NYOS SC 2002
Sophie Bancroft	'Dreams of a Prairie Sea'	NYJOS Summer 2002

APPENDIX 6

Bill Wells	'The Man I Love/Of Thee I Sing'	NYJOS Summer 2002
Malcolm Edmonstone	'The Poplar/That Time Again'	NYJOS Summer 2002
Aidan O'Donnell	'I'd Love To . . .'	NYJOS Summer 2002
Phil Bancroft	'Colour Theory'	NYJOS Summer 2002
Sally Beamish	Trumpet Concerto	NYOS SC 2003

APPENDIX 6

The National Youth Orchestras of Scotland: CD Recordings

NYOS 001
THE NATIONAL YOUTH ORCHESTRA OF SCOTLAND
Conductor: Christopher Seaman
Soloist: Ernst Kovacic
Thomas Wilson, Violin Concerto (NYOS commission with funds provided by BP)
Shostakovich, Festival Overture Op. 96
Holst, *Planets* Suite: Mars, Jupiter, Saturn, Uranus

NYOS 002
CAMERATA SCOTLAND (NYOS CHAMBER ORCHESTRA)
Conductor: William Conway
Mozart, Symphony No. 29 in A
Beethoven, Symphony No. 2 in D

NYOS 003
CAMERATA SCOTLAND
Conductor: William Conway
Soloist: Colette Ruddy (mezzo soprano)
Mendelssohn, Symphony No. 3 'Scottish'
Thomson, *Three Lieder*
Thomson, Overture to *Hermann*

NYOS 004
NATIONAL YOUTH ORCHESTRA OF SCOTLAND
Conductor: Bramwell Tovey
Soloist: Michael Thompson
Thea Musgrave, Horn Concerto
Elgar, Symphony No. 1 Op. 55

NYOS 005
THE NATIONAL YOUTH JAZZ ORCHESTRA OF SCOTLAND
Featuring jazz composer/performer Nikki Yeoh and the work 'Quiet Freedom'
    (commissioned by NYOS)

NYOS 006
THE NATIONAL YOUTH ORCHESTRA OF SCOTLAND
Conductor: Junichi Hirokami
Rory Boyle, *Capriccio* (commissioned by NYOS)
Conductor: Bramwell Tovey
Gustav Holst, *The Perfect Fool*
Conductor: Takuo Yuasa
Wagner, Prelude to *Die Meistersinger*
Ravel, *Daphnis and Chloe* Orchestral Suites No. 1 and 2

APPENDIX 7

Honorary Presidents of NYOS

Sir Alexander Gibson 1979–95
Emeritus Professor Donald Pack, CBE 1988–

APPENDIX 8

Trustees of the NYOS Endowment Trust

Viscount Younger KT KCVO TD DL   1991–2002
Dr Richard Ellis OBE DL MA LLB LLD (Hon)   1991–
Mr Colin MacLean MA   1991–

Sir Thomas Risk BL LLD (Hon) FRSE	1991–7
Dr David Robertson CBE MA MEd	1991–8
Sir John Shaw CBE	1998–
Dr Norman Cooper PhD MBA FI Mgt	1998–
Mr Iain Harrison CBE	2002–
Professor Ewan Brown CBE	2003

APPENDIX 9

Members of NYOS Council

Professor Donald Pack CBE 1978–95
David Robertson 1978–98
Denis O'Riordan MBE 1978–95
Richard Evans 1978–94
Colin MacLean 1978–94
June Lady Aberdeen CBE 1978–94
Kirsty Adam 1978–92
Martin Dalby 1978–92
James Clark 1978–91
Herrick Bunney MVO 1978–89
Councillor John Campbell 1978–87
Peter Donald MBE 1978–87
Michael Storrs 1978–85
Anthony Willcocks 1978–84
Sir David Lumsden 1978–83
David Richardson 1978–82
Councillor W. J. Taylor 1978–81
Helen Davidson 1978–
Fiona Grant 1981–5
Geoffrey Phillips 1982–7
Jack Jenkins 1983–8
Councillor Bernard Scott 1983–7
John Boyle 1983–6
Sir Philip Ledger CBE 1985–97
Ian Ritchie 1985–93
John Hughes 1985–7
Councillor James Burns 1986–93
Councillor G. D. Swapp 1986–9
Stephen Carpenter 1986–8
Ian Sandison 1987–90
Raymond Brookes 1987–2002
Alastair Beattie 1988–96
Dr Ian Laing 1989–99

Councillor Robins 1989–90
Dr Norman Cooper 1989–
Iain Harrison CBE 1990–9
Councillor Ronald Forbes 1991–4
Ronald Walker 1991–3
David Harding OBE 1991–2
Alan Simpson 1992–
Simon Miller 1993–7
Councillor Barry McCulloch 1993–6
Judy Steel 1993–6
Neil Munro 1994–7
Timothy Laing 1994–
Alex Perry 1994–
Councillor Margaret Howe 1995–2000
Grant Baird 1995–8
Maggi Allan 1996–2002
Ian Smith 1996–2000
Councillor Alan Dick 1996–8
Michael Pell 1996–
Eddie Friel 1997–2000
Neil Meldrum 1997–
Geoffrey Lord OBE 1998–
Graeme Wilson 1998–
Robert Manson 2000–
Councillor Maira Martin 2000–
Lord Robert McLennan of Rogart 2000–
Douglas Millar 2000–
Tony Vogt 2000–
Douglas Fairley 2001–
Elspeth Orcharton 2001–
Professor Gary Roach 2001–
John Wallace OBE 2002–
Robin Pagett 2002–

APPENDIX 10

The National Youth Orchestra of Scotland: Ensemble Tutors

STRINGS
Julian Clayton
William Conway
James Durrant
Martin Hughes
Peter Jones
Peter Mountain
Clive Thomas
Geoffrey Trabichoff

WOODWIND
Donald Finlayson
Alan Garner
Sheena Gordon
Geoffrey Haydock
Philip Hill
Robin Miller
Michael Norris
Alison Waller
Edgar Williams

BRASS
Bryan Allan
Nigel Boddice
David Flack
Charles Floyd
Lance Green
Ian Smith
Maurice Temple
Kevin Thompson

PERCUSSION
Lachlan Birch
Glynn Bragg
Ian Coulter
Ruaridh Donaldson
Pamela Dow
Martin Gibson
Eric Hendry
David Lyons

APPENDIX 11

The National Youth Orchestra of Scotland: Orchestra Managers and Heads of House Staff

ORCHESTRA MANAGERS

Stephen McGhee	1979–85
Christopher Foster	1986
William McDonald	1987
Iain Campbell	1988–97
Thomas Hattrick	1998–2001
Trevor Marshall	2002
David O'Connell	2002
Andrew Langford	2002–3

HEADS OF HOUSE STAFF

Jean Wainwright	1979–92
James Wainwright	1979–81
Arthur Ross	1980–91
James Wilkinson	1981–4
Rosamund Beveridge	1992–8
Elizabeth Bragg	1993
Chris O'Grady	1994
Sue O'Grady	1996–2000
Nicholas Smith	1999–

Appendix 12

The National Youth Orchestra of Scotland: Student Exchanges

STUDENTS TO NYOS

Summer Course 1992	Bjarte Mo (violin) NORWAY
Winter Course 1992–3	Chie Arakawa (double bass) JAPAN
Summer Course 1993	Asne Volle (cello) NORWAY
Winter Course 1993–4	Chiho Yoshikoshi (violin) JAPAN Schubert Christy (violin)

	INDONESIA
	Anna Malkin (violin)
	USA
Winter Course 1994–5	Justina Allocca (violin)
	USA
	Rebecca Taylor (violin)
	AUSTRALIA
	Itziar Prieto (violin)
	SPAIN
	Laura Salcedo (violin)
	SPAIN
Summer Course 1996	Rachel Wile (violin)
	USA
Winter Course 1997–8	Esther Augustinovicz (violin)
	HUNGARY
	Birgit Leitner (viola)
	AUSTRIA
Winter Course 1998–9	Geraldine O'Doherty (harp)
	DUBLIN
	Bertin Christelbauer (cello)
	AUSTRIA
	Pia Grassl (cello)
	AUSTRIA
Summer Course 1999	Sally Richards (harp)
	WILTSHIRE
Summer Course 2000	Geraldine O'Doherty (harp)
	DUBLIN
Winter Course 2000–1	David Buosso (violin)
	NEW YORK
	Ramzi Hussein (viola)
	PALESTINE
Summer Course 2001	Cristian Gonzalez (violin)
	CHILE
	Alexandra Brown (viola)
	FRANCE
	Stephanie Beck (harp)
	LIECHTENSTEIN
Winter Course 2001–2	Stephanie Beck (harp)
	LIECHTENSTEIN
Winter Course 2002–3	Stephanie Beck (harp)
	LIECHTENSTEIN
	Eva Gerard (viola)
	USA

STUDENTS FROM NYOS

April 1991	
	Shelagh Walker (cello)
	JAPAN
March/April 1992	Gillianne Haddow (viola)
	JAPAN

Appendix 12

May/June 1995	Clare Sargent (cello) NEW YORK
August/September 1996	Lisa Davidson (viola) AUSTRALIA
March 1997	Simone Welsh (violin) Rebecca Savage (double bass) SPAIN
May/June 1997	Christopher Gray (double bass) NEW YORK
January–June 1998	Emma Smith (double bass) ITALY
March 1998	Iona Hassan (violin) Murray Fergusson (violin) AUSTRIA
July 1998	Katie Duffy (violin) SPAIN
September 1998	James Cheek (oboe) Jenni Cooper (bassoon) MALAYSIA
June 1999	Ruth Lunny (violin) SPAIN
August/September 1999	Jenny Davie (violin) BELGIUM
May/June 2001	Katie Bell (cello) NEW YORK
August 2001	Carol Ripley (violin) JAPAN
August/September 2001	Lorna John (oboe) BELGIUM
September 2002	Soraya Khan (violin) Amanda Babington (violin) Nicola Bates (violin) Heather Kennedy (violin) SPAIN

CAMERATA SCOTLAND

Summer 1997	Philip Dawson (double bass) Matthew Midgley (double bass) Thomas Lowe (trumpet) ENGLAND Barbara Kehrig (bassoon) GERMANY Eamonn Nolan (trumpet) IRELAND
Summer 1999	Richard Freeman (trumpet) ENGLAND

APPENDIX 13

Awards and Prizes

WINNERS OF THE LASMO STAFFA MUSIC AWARD

1993	Gareth Small	Trumpet	Royal Academy of Music
1994	Colette Ruddy	Mezzo soprano	Royal Scottish Academy of Music and Drama
1995	Tómas Tómasson	Bass	Royal College of Music
1996	Ekaterina Apekisheva	Piano	Royal Scottish Academy of Music and Drama
1997	Andrew Haveron	Violin	Royal College of Music
1998	Corina Belcea	Violin	Royal College of Music
1999	Marko Martin	Piano	Guildhall School of Music and Drama
2000	Marina Nadiradze	Piano	Royal Scottish Academy of Music and Drama
2001	Nadja Zwiener	Violin	Guildhall School of Music and Drama

WINNERS OF THE LASMO STAFFA SINGER'S PRIZE

1998	Leigh Melrose	Baritone	Royal Academy of Music
1999	Timothy Mirfin	Bass	Royal Academy of Music
2000	Jonathan Lemalu	Bass	Royal College of Music

WINNER OF NYOS STAFFA AWARD

2002	Wouter Raubenheimer	Viola	Royal Scottish Academy of Music and Drama

Index

157

INDEX